MULTI-LEVEL M

THE COMPLETE GUIDE TO GENERATING, CLOSING & WORKING WITH ALL THE PEOPLE YOU NEED TO MAKE *REAL* MONEY *EVERY* MONTH IN NETWORK MARKETING

Dr. Jeffrey Lant

Published by JLA Publications
A Division of Jeffrey Lant Associates, Inc.
P.O. Box 38-2767
Cambridge, MA 02238
(617) 547-6372

MULTI-LEVEL MONEY

The Complete Guide To Generating, Closing & Working With All The People You Need To Make *Real* Money *Every* Month In Network Marketing

Dr. Jeffrey Lant

Dedication:

I dedicate this book to George Kosch, my Canadian colleague and pal, who has, with his voyages through mastery and of the Internet helped me create and manage my pace-setting "Money Mall", opening up the staggering potential of cyber-profit to network marketers worldwide.

CONTENTS

INTRODUCTION

Welcome to the new Second Edition of this book. Thousands of people in virtually all existing network marketing companies in this country and abroad are now profiting from this resource. I regularly hear from them as they write telling me how they're using these techniques — day in, day out — to build larger, more profitable organizations. Good for them. Their demonstrated success is one very good reason I know these techniques work. A second is that I use them myself, every single day, to build a larger pay-check for myself every 30 days.

Do you get a raise from your job every 30 days? Probably not. But I do. Every four weeks when the checks arrive from the MLM companies I'm involved with, I get further proof that these techniques work well, indeed *very* well. MLM has never been a full-time job for me; (it's a part-time, home-based business for me, just as it is for most of my readers). Nonetheless, working part-time, I earn much more than many full-time professionals in well-paying fields. That is as it should be.

I hasten to add that my success in MLM, now amptly demonstrated, was neither effortless nor inevitable. It came about because I learned from my uncertain beginnings. I took the time to analyze what went wrong with my early efforts and to keep plugging away until two things happened: I learned that if you're going to be successful in MLM the people in your downline must be successful... and that the only way they're going to be successful is by having a profit-making *system* they can easily understand and duplicate in their daily efforts.

In each of my three unsuccessful involvements in MLM this didn't happen.

The first time I got involved in MLM, for instance, was many years ago, in one of those ubiquitous diet-powder companies. It was virtually a parody of what a sensible MLM company should be, albeit all too typical. The executives were egregiously self-serving; they never gave a moment's thought to how their independent distributors should recruit other distributors, much less to how they should retain them. The result was predictable: within well under a year this well-publicized enterprise was a smouldering ruin. How could it have been otherwise? Deduction: avoid all MLM companies where there is no *system* for success, where the executives are not 100% dedicated to creating and maintaining such a system.

The second time I put a toe in the water, I got involved with one of the industry gurus you read about. He at least had a glimmering that a system was necessary for success. Unfortunately, his had so many holes in it you could drive a coach and six through them. Moreover, it was ridiculously complicated and difficult to understand. More, it was distinctly unappreciated by the parent company which wanted its distributors to sell its products door to door, just as they'd always done and in no other ways. Instead of a unified, company-endorsed, systematic success system designed to recruit and retain independent distributors, there was petty, internecine warfare. In short order, I walked. (So did the guru, by the way. Ultimately, he went to another company where he implemented his "system." It didn't work there, either, and as a result he says he's never gonna be an independent distributor ever, ever again! Actually, he just drew the wrong conclusion from the evidence. He needed more responsive companies to work with and a far easier, "distributor friendly" marketing system.)

Deduction: avoid half-baked, complicated "systems" and parent companies that don't support even these. Walk through any "guru's" system and see if it makes sense, if you can do it, if it works. If not, don't bite. It'll be trouble in the long run.

Fast forward years ahead. I'd decided that while the basic concept of MLM was certainly valid and intriguing (people recruiting people who recruit people who recruit people, each subsequent person providing profit for their upline), the execution left a lot to be desired. However, I let myself be persuaded to try once more.

This time I got involved with a company that fit in with the overall theme of my Sure-Fire Business Success Catalog. I thought I could easily sell the program through my catalog, card deck, *etc*. And so it proved. I had no problem signing up people and in short order became a top distributor in the company, making pretty good money.

Unfortunately, I had lots of problems keeping my recruits in the company. The reason, of course, was that the company had no duplicatable system. It was nothing more than a revolving door.

In my perhaps naive enthusiasm I thought the company CEO would want to change this, would at least understand the benefits of keeping people in his company and do everything to help them succeed. Silly me! This CEO, despite an ocean of rhetoric to the contrary (he specialized in sick-making "I really want to help you" dialogue), had only one person in mind: himself. And since the system he'd instituted feathered his own nest so very well, he was uninterested in helping other people. He benefited from the monthly fees and by selling overpriced marketing communications, prospect leads, and "training" aids. The fact that the vast majority of people in his company not only didn't make money but were virtually certain to lose it, didn't seem to bother him at all. The Alfred E. Newman of network marketing, he lived by the "What me worry?" principle. And after I came into the company — bringing with me a ton of people — he probably rubbed his hands in glee since it daily meant more money for him — and no reason to change whatsoever.

Unfortunately, things didn't work out quite so easily, as Mr. "#1 Uber Alles" quickly learned. You see, I had no intention of allowing my name to be used to bring people into an enterprise that was doomed. I therefore insisted that he develop a *system* for independent distributor recruitment and retention — or else, I'd do it myself. He didn't — or wouldn't — do it. So I did. And I got daily evidence that the kind of systematic procedures I bring to every aspect of my business life produced the same kind of beneficial results in MLM.

In short order I produced for my organization a host of crucial prospect-generating and business-building tools, including:

- inexpensive self-mailer marketing communications, where the message about the company's benefits and the benefits of my group were fully presented and where the document would still mail for the cost of a first-class postage stamp
- a regular supply of prospect leads
- telemarketing assistance
- a downline newsletter with marketing tips, *etc.*

In sum, I started to act like the company and its CEO should have acted... but were either unable or unwilling to do so.

Was the company CEO delighted about these distributor-centered reforms? Not on your life. When I created inexpensive marketing communications, it destroyed a profit center for him. He'd been gouging his members for expensive four-color printing, *etc.* Now they could get better, more complete, easier to work with and more persuasive marketing materials imprinted with their name, address, phone number, and company i.d. for far less than they'd been paying — materials, too, they could mail for less. They were happy. The CEO fumed.

By the same token, the CEO had been selling prospect leads for several times what we could provide them for. We wanted people to have as many good, inexpensive leads as they could work. He wanted to profit just by selling the leads. Unsurprisingly, when my service creamed his, another income source was destroyed. Again, he fumed.

My marketing oriented monthly newsletter provided detailed tips on how to recruit and retain members. By contrast, his company publication didn't have information on either of these subjects. In fact, it actually talked about the lavish lifestyle of the CEO and featured his mug several times in any given issue. I told him he should be talking about things that were exclusively of use to the distributors and stop talking about himself all the time. But he was always in this for *himself*, and it always showed. Actions always speak louder than words, and his actions screamed, "Me! Me! Me!" Revolting.

Unsurprisingly, as people in the company learned about my system and how it worked, they wanted it. In fact, many emphatically demanded to be placed in my organization and so my numbers grew in this way, too, until I had well over half of the company under me. Remember, I started with zero. But here's something you should know: smart people always prefer a profitable system to anarchy and organizational vacuum. Always.

By now, of course, my initially amiable relations with the company CEO were history. His one idea seemed to be that he'd exploit me and my name to his continuing advantage, that he could continue to run his entirely self-serving system, ignoring the independent distributors while telling them every chance he got what a big wheel he was and how lucky they were to be associated with him. Needless to say I didn't see things this way at all.

To me, the job of an MLM company CEO is clear:

1) keep the company on the competitive edge;

2) run it efficiently and competently;

3) pay monies owed on time, and

4) do everything possible to assist independent distributors to recruit and retain other independent distributors and achieve maximum success.

If this isn't happening in a company — no matter how "famous" — it's time to get out and go where it is happening.

And that, in due course, is precisely what I did.

Disgusted as I was with this rapacious, self-serving and unintelligent CEO, I was ecstatic that 1) I'd gotten out and that 2) I'd discovered — proven to my complete satisfaction — that you can make money in network marketing if the four basic conditions listed above are present. Now the question was, what company offered these conditions?

Well, friend, into each life come moments of what the Arabs felicitously call "kismet," fate. And so it happened with me. While I was still very much immersed in the murky affairs of my third network marketing company, I was diagnosed as a diabetic. Like most diabetics (before they start taking care of themselves), I was overweight and I suffered the usual consequences, being sluggish, having too little energy, eating the wrong things, *etc*. Once I'd been diagnosed, however, I did what every person should do (and much earlier than it dawned on me): I took personal responsibility for my health — for the first time in my life.

While doing so, I had the supreme good fortune to come across a man and a company that literally changed my life, not just my business life but, in the most fundamental way, my entire life. The man is Don Smyth, his company is The Staff of Life — and I shall always be grateful to them both.

You'll learn more about Don Smyth and The Staff of Life later. For now, suffice it to say that he had the kind of rock-solid, cutting-edge company I wanted, with products that made a significant difference in the lives of real people. He was awesomely well-organized and completely dedicted to the kind of flawless customer service that I thought no longer existed, anywhere. All of this was captivating, and I joined up with my pal Robert Blackman, who also knew a good thing when he saw it.

From the very beginning we were successful. Indeed, the thing worked like a charm:

- people understood they had health problems and health needs
- they were willing, often anxious to try the products
- once they'd tried the products, they bought them (most through the monthly Insured Program, whereby they purchase a certain quantity every 30 days)
- while some simply stayed on as happy consumers, others (the more entrepreneurial) started selling The Staff of Life as a business opportunity, building, as Robert and I were doing, a growing long-term income, not just looking for a few quick bucks.

With The Staff of Life, we got the chance not only to implement our complete recruitment and retention system with our own group but with the company overall. Don Smyth, you see, was the first network marketing CEO to retain us to bring our system to the entire company, tens of thousands of members. Result? Almost every single month is a record sales month these days at The Staff of Life, as the company moves ahead in lock-step progression from success to success. And, of course, the monthly pay-checks of The Lant/Blackman Better Health Team keep on moving ahead smartly, too, bigger every month — just as they're supposed to be.

I owe Don Smyth and The Staff of Life a lot. Thanks to their fine products (I take five every day) which I use along with a sensible health regime, I'm back to my old college weight, looking and feeling terrific; I'm almost 50 now and have no problem passing for Jack Benny's "39", or less. Too, I've found a company that I intend to promote for life and, along with Robert Blackman, build to gigantic proportions, with our growing monthly pay-checks to match.

I've also shown that when the four key variables listed above are in place, network marketing makes sense as an income source. I've shown that making money in MLM isn't merely a function of how early you get into a company and having to rip off people. I've proven that dedicated CEOs and companies can add, at reasonable cost, an independent distributor recruitment and retention program that makes sense for everyone — CEO, company, and all independent distributors. And I've put the stupid, self-centered, rapacious CEOs of other companies on notice that the self-serving and self-defeating ways they run their businesses are no longer acceptable.

You see, one of the things that's going to happen when you read this book is that you will put your current MLM "opportunity" under a microscope. Just as when you did so in Biology I in high school with some specimen, you may not like what you see very much. Good. Human time is too precious to waste a moment. And if the company you're with now doesn't measure up and won't work with you, get out.

By the same token, you'll analyze under that same microscope any new "opportunities" you're thinking about. Good. Now you have the tools you need to know if you're going to be successful in a network marketing opportunity or not — before you take the plunge.

Finally, you know that you can always join the opportunities I recommend and work myself. I'm not experimenting any more in MLM. I've got a system that works. This system is available to you, too. You can get it in The Staff of Life, of course. It's also available with The Gourmet Coffee Club, too, an easy, smart program designed to cash in on the fact that more than 100,000,000 Americans drink coffee every single day... with many times that drinking coffee abroad. (Yes, GCC, like The Staff of Life, is an international program, and I personally have distributors in many countries.) And you can get it, too in my other recommended opportunities, too, a complete list of which you can always get by calling me at (617) 547-6372 or dropping me a note.

You see, you can successfully take my system into *any* company that meets the four key criteria listed above. Thus, you can diversify your empire and your income, while decreasing the risk that's always a part of business.

This system — which I call "The Awesome Power of One" — is simple and sensible. Take a look at the chart below.

It clearly demonstrates that if you recruit just one person per month and that each of these recruits just one person per month for one year, you'll end up at the end of the 12th month with over 2,000 people in your organization. See for yourself...

# of distributors	month	# of distributors	month
1	1	64	7
2	2	128	8
4	3	256	9
8	4	512	10
16	5	1024	11
32	6	2048	12

A Few Key Points About This Chart

i) At six months, you have only about 1.5% of the downline organization you'll have after a year. Don't be discouraged by this. As you see, the dramatic growth comes shortly. Unfortunately, in network marketing, most people are out of a program long before the 6th month, so they never benefit from the exponential growth.

ii) you'll probably lose money for the first 4-6 months. We all know the old saw that it "takes money to make money." Nowhere is this more true than in MLM. It'll cost you money to join your program, pay monthly fees, pay for marketing materials, get leads, follow them up, etc. However, if your organization is doubling monthly, that's what you should be focused on. The minimal amount of money you spend in the first six months will be offset by the substantial amount of money you make afterwards.

iii) the doubling doesn't stop at 12 months! The methods that have brought you this degree of success, are the methods you must continue to use thereafter for even greater rewards.

To make this system work, the company has to do its part by maintaining its competitive position with its products and services, handling central administration and payments expeditiously and ensuring that it does its part to help the independent distributors recruit and retain members.

To make this system work, you've got to do your part. You've got to put in the time, money, energy and other resources necessary to make it work. You've got to shuck any "get rich quick" sentiments you may have and be willing to do what it takes to succeed in any business: set a personal goal, have specific objectives, invest what it takes to succeed, work assiduously, remain patient, and, always, evaluate what works (so you can do more of it) and what doesn't (so you can stop).

To make this system work, the people you recruit have got to do their part. The curious, infuriating notion exists in network marketing that you can sign up and do nothing. Well, that's just plain stupid. No one in any other business believes that; you cannot believe that here, either. Success takes work — by the company, by you, by the people you recruit, by the people they recruit, *etc*. Network marketing would be a breeze if people understood this fact and acted on it. Instead, the industry is filled with the slothful, the inefficient, the disorganized, the rapacious, the stupid, and those who pride themselves not merely on being these things, but wishing to stay these things.

I'm not one of these people, and you can't be one of them, either. And after you absorb this book and its revolutionary methods you won't be. For make no mistake about it, what you're about to read is not the standard way business in done in the network marketing industry. It's not the way anyone in the first three "opportunities"

I got involved with did business, and it's not the way their colleagues generally do business. But it's the way sensible, solid people like Don Smyth (CEO, The Staff of Life), Col. Bill Blaesing (CEO, Gourmet Coffee Club), and Ed Freeman (CEO, The World's Largest Permanent Downline) do business.

I take my hat off to these people. And I will take it off to you, too. Let me know how you're doing in MLM, how these methods work for you, just like thousands of people already do, who read this book, my network marketing special reports and articles, and pay close attention to my MLM training videos.

And, remember, I'm not just writing about these techniques. *I'm living them.* Sadly, you'll find there are a host of so-called MLM experts in this country and abroad who think there is nothing incongruous about being unable to make money themselves in MLM by establishing a successful, profit-making recruiting and retention system but continuing to write about how others should do it. I find that despicable, of course, and absurb. I want you to know that my colleague Robert Blackman and I are in the trenches just like you, working every day, just like you've got to do, to implement this system and improve it and to build larger monthly income for ourselves. We don't just talk the talk. And I warn you, I won't let you do that, either. We follow the techniques in this book *every single day* — just as you'll want to do, if you truly wish to succeed to the maximum extent possible.

A Look At The Contents

This book is composed of 6 chapters.

Chapter 1 takes up the question of how to select the right network marketing company. Most people seem to select a network marketing company with a complete absence of critical intelligence. But not YOU! This chapter supplies the tough questions you've got to ask — and get answered. You can't make any money if you select the wrong company. Now you shouldn't make that mistake.

In **Chapter 2** you learn about The L.A.N.T. SYSTEM™ (Lucrative Advancements in Networking Tactics), the system that makes me money in MLM. The real problem with virtually all network marketing companies is that once you're recruited they leave you on your own. *They* focus on the *products* and on squeezing as much money out of *you* as possible. You're left to figure out all the essentials of money-making marketing. This is ridiculous. The only company you should affiliate with is one that's committed to supporting you as an independent distributor. That's where The L.A.N.T. SYSTEM™ comes in. It's composed of three major elements: generating all the leads you and members of your organization need; using client-centered, benefit-rich marketing communications (particularly the "self-mailers" you're going to learn about) to approach them, and having effective telemarketing support available. In short, doing *everything* necessary to support the independent distributor. After you read this Chapter, you'll realize how bereft of marketing intelligence most network marketing companies are... and you'll never accept their lack of independent distributor support as a given.

Friend, with this book a new day dawns in network marketing. No longer will it be acceptable merely to sponsor independent distributors — and ignore them. No longer will they take this unsatisfactory state of affairs as a given. From now on, distributors will demand real company support and a system that works. This book will ensure it. Why? Because after this book becomes known, companies really interested in assisting the independent distributor will do so, implementing this system. Others, run by the profoundly, impenetrably stupid won't. As a result, they'll be increasingly ignored by distributors who, intelligently, will go where their chances of success are enhanced.

Chapter 3 moves on to deal with lead generation. You cannot succeed in network marketing... and your downline members cannot succeed... if you all don't have a constant flow of high-quality prospect leads. This chapter shows you how to get them!

Chapter 4 shows you how to get ready to handle the responses once you've got them. It's amazing to me how lax people are about the preparation for prompt and timely lead response. Generating leads is never enough for success... you've got to evaluate them properly and follow up appropriately. This chapter tells you how to do both.

In **Chapter 5** you learn how to get your new distributors off to a profitable start. Industry studies show that the average independent network marketing distributor sponsors no more than two people in any given opportunity. In this chapter, you'll learn how to sponsor that minimum number in the first thirty days alone — thereafter maintaining a continuing recruitment program, an essential if you are going to make real money.

Chapter 6 carries on the discussion by showing you just what you've got to do to work with your distributors week in, week out so that they produce both for themselves and for you. This important topic of independent distributor maintenance and support is widely overlooked in the industry literature, but unless you succeed in this area you cannot make network marketing profitable. It's as simple as that.

Additional appendices provide:

▌ crucial step-by-step details on how to use leveraging to build a supremely large, profitable organization;

▌ additional resources to assist you build your organization, and

▌ further information and sign-up details about several companies which already have in place the unrelenting independent distributor centered recruitment and retention techniques recommended in this book. Yes, you can use this resource to become successful in *any* MLM company, but if the company you're in won't assist you in this process, the march to success is needlessly complicated and takes lots longer. If you don't want that, join me in companies that already "get it," understanding that they, too, have a crucial role to play in your success.

A Few Words About Your Author: Dr. Jeffrey Lant

First, you need to understand that I'm not an armchair theorist; I'm a guy with *very big expectations*. Network marketing is not my full-time job, although I make more than a full-time income from it. I have lots of other things on my plate. That's why I worked so hard to create a *system* that ensures success. I don't have a minute to waste. Neither do you!

Second, I always play to win. I didn't get into MLM to "make a few bucks." I make more than a "few bucks" every single day already. I got into MLM to exploit to the max its international leveraging possibilities. I don't do well with people who set tiny limits on themselves, who have no glorious expectations for themselves and won't do what's necessary to achieve them. This is an activist's book. It demands that you think! Plan! Act! Rethink! And keep on keepin' on, improving things as you go! Just as I do. I was gifted with amazing energy (which has been noticeably improved by The Staff of Life products I take). This energy is placed at creating the most lucrative system possible... and working that system... and working it some more!

Third, I am a marketer, not just a network marketer. Let me explain what that means. I am in the business of helping anyone sell anything. I have spent many years studying just what it takes to get the human animal to take action to acquire something. I am fascinated by the marketing game, by the transfer of items of value for products and services which the purchaser wishes to acquire. It is an unendingly fascinating game.

Over the course of many years, I have created many vehicles to assist people win the marketing game.

— there are my many marketing books. Flip to the back cover of this resource and you'll see a number of them. All are unrelentingly detailed, packed with techniques you can use RIGHT NOW to move your product or your service and achieve maximum success. The hallmark of any Lant book — including this one — is LIFETIME VALUE.

— there are my articles and Special Reports. Busy people don't always have time to read a long, detailed book; they want specific, useful information fast. That's why I write hundreds of specialized business articles and Special Reports. My articles reach over 1.5 million people monthly in both print and electronic database formats. A complete list of my Special Reports is available through my free quarterly Sure-Fire Business Success Catalog. Call to get your subscription started.

— there's my quarterly 100,000 circulation Sales & Marketing Success Card Deck. If you're real keen on succeeding in network marketing (or if you have other products and services you want to sell nationally), you'll be in this deck some day, the sooner the better. Why? Because it can provide you — for the lowest prices in the entire industry — with an avalanche of prospect leads every 90 days; you'll use these leads to build your organization — without spending very much money yourself. (Dozens of smart marketers have written to thank me specifically for the detailed leveraging techniques you're about to read saying that these alone as worth many times the cost of this book. They're right. And the sooner you start using them, the sooner your dramatic organizational growth will take place.)

— there's my National Copywriting Center. *Everyone* in business (*whatever* the business) needs marketing communications that get real people to bite, to sit up and take notice and act, either to identify themselves as a prospect or to actually buy what you're selling. The sad truth is, most marketing communications do not begin to do this necessary job; they're a complete waste of time and money. Not what we produce. Our marketing communications are stark, simple, motivating, fast-moving — and reasonably priced. The way they ought to be. When you're in the market for prospect and buyer *action* and need marketing communications that deliver your message and motivate action, call me. We can create a turn-key marketing *system* for you that will help you generate prospect leads, turn them into buyers, and maintain your profitable relationship with them for years. We'll conceive, write, edit, design and print *whatever you want* — whenever you want it.

There's alot more to JLA, but you can see for yourself by requesting my Sure-Fire Business Success Catalog. What you need to keep in mind is one basic thing: we help serious people make serious money. It's as simple as that. And now that's what you're going to get in this straightforward, tested, ultra-practical book.

The insistent, hard-hitting, practical, "do it now," "telling it like it is" presentation is going to upset some people. I can't help that. Life isn't a walk in the park. Achieving success in anything isn't effortless. It can't be done with a vacuum for a brain. It isn't going to come to the "little guys" who keep thinking like "little guys." And it certainly is never going to come to those who won't plan for success, know the game they're playing, hard-headedly examine their options, and do what's necessary to succeed. They may talk about success... but that's as close as they'll get to it. That's not me. And I trust it isn't you. You want maximum success. You want to know how to get it. You've come to me for practical assistance. And, by God, I'm determined to provide it.

So without further ado, I give you a resource and hundreds of techniques that can change your life and bring you an income through MLM that can grow every 30 days for the rest of your life so long as your company, the people you recruit and you yourself work together to implement the system that is now at your fingertips.

Cambridge, MA

CHAPTER 1

FINDING THE RIGHT NETWORK MARKETING OPPORTUNITY, THE OPPORTUNITY THAT WILL WORK WITH YOU AND MAKE YOU MONEY

If you want a successful outcome, you must be certain you have the right ingredients. Frankly, one of the reasons so many people fail in network marketing is because they didn't do their homework, didn't join the right opportunity. Face it: if you join the wrong opportunity, the opportunity that doesn't make distributor development a priority, you are going to fail. That's why research is not a luxury, but a necessity.

Thus, before joining any business opportunity, review several. Do so in a systematic way to ensure that you're comparing apples to apples. Here's how to handle the review process:

1) Gather all your details as promptly as possible during a defined period. Don't drag out the process of selecting an opportunity. At any given time there are a variety of good opportunities on the market. What you've got to do is analyze all of them and make a commitment to just one of them.

Note: If you're not really certain that operating a business, working a business opportunity is for you, do yourself and everyone else a favor: don't even get started. One of the most frustrating thing for people selling a business opportunity is encountering the "looker", the "wannabee", the person who thinks he wants an opportunity but really isn't sure. These people are killers. They waste millions of dollars every year by sending in coupons and answering ads for opportunities they really have no interest in working. Don't be this way. If you seriously want an opportunity, be serious in your approach to the subject. If you don't, please find another way of occupying your time, because you're a real menace in this field if you're not committed to finding a business opportunity and making it work.

2) Put all your materials in one place. Finding the opportunity you can commit yourself to uses some of the same skills you'll use to make that opportunity a success.

You've got to be disciplined, efficient, and organized. One aspect of this means putting all your business opportunity information in a place where you can easily find it. One significant mistake business opportunity seekers make is looking at opportunities one by one. They'll request information, review it, and discard it... then go on to repeat the process, often dozens of times. This is ridiculous. You've got to be able to *compare* opportunities. This means keeping all your information in one, easily accessible spot.

3) Create a comparison questionnaire. After you've got your material, start comparing what the different opportunities offer. You can use this handy questionnaire:

name of opportunity_____ address _____

telephone _____ contact person _____

year founded _____ chief product line _____

How would I distribute product?

Does company offer entirely replicatable sales/recruitment program?

If so, how does it work? If not, how do they expect me to recruit?

What price does company charge for its marketing communications and sales materials? Can these be customized with my printed name, address, phone, fax?

If so, at what cost?

Does company offer its program and materials on interactive computer diskette?

How much does it cost to ship recommended materials to each prospect?

How does company expect me to get leads to sell products/opportunity to?

Does company prohibit me from joining lead-generating programs such as Ad-Net, Inc.?

Does company offer any advertising subsidies?

Does company offer telemarketing support? If so, how?

Does company offer training materials to succeed as an independent distributor? If so, on what basis?

Does company offer periodic training courses?

If so, when and on what basis?

Does company offer "hot-line" assistance for distributors? If so, during what hours?

What is the financial condition of the company? How do I know?

How much debt is it carrying?

How does company compensate independent distributors?

<If there are more ways than one for you to make money in this opportunity, list them here and list precisely what compensation you'd receive. Be realistic! This is an easy place to get overly enthusiastic!>

Is there a monthly payment? If so, how much?

How many people do I have to recruit, or at what point do I break even and start to make money?

Does the company pay in a timely fashion?

Has there been any difficulty with timely payment?

How successful is my upline sponsor? Does he seem to understand how to make money with this company? What is his current position?

What kind of assistance is he offering?

What about the overall group that I'm joining? Is it active/successful?

Does company require some or all of the following:

 — attendance at regular meetings

 — door-to-door solicitation

 — organizing local "house parties"

 — storing products

 — minimum product purchases (if so, how much?)

Do I want to do these things?

In priority order what are the five most persuasive reasons for joining this company?

1)

2)

3)

4)

5)

(If you have had poor results with a previous business opportunity.)

What is different about this business opportunity that will help me avoid the problems I've experienced in the past?

This questionnaire may look formidable, but the truth is, as an independent distributor for any company you need to have this information... and when you're a distributor you're going to get all the answers soon enough. Problem is, if you don't know what you're facing in advance, you may not like the answers very much.

Try to remember that 98%+ of people going into a business opportunity, whether networking marketing or not, fail. They fail for many reasons, but one of the leading reasons why they fail is because they don't really know what they're getting into and don't have the business skills and financial resources to make a success of their undertaking.

You'd think, of course, that this high distributor failure rate would alarm people selling the opportunity, but I don't think it fazes them in the least. Why? Because sellers of opportunities can still make money — often lots of money — even if you fail!

How's that again?

Easy! When you join a company, you're probably going to be required to pay for some or all of the following:

- registration fee

- advance payment for first month or quarter

- sample pack

- minimum product inventory

- marketing communications like cards, stationery, post-cards, brochures, business plans, various re-prints, *etc.*

Keep in mind that the company makes money on ALL of these things... so that they are profitable whether you make a dime or not. Company executives reckon that they can do very well, thank you, just by selling these items. Thus, they don't have to be too worried about your success. If you succeed, if, that is, you sell product and recruit additional distributors, so much the better. That's a real benefit to the company. But if you don't, no problem; you've still contributed to the company's annual revenues.

Because the failure rate is so high for people running opportunities, and because the system is so heavily weighted against the independent distributor and in favor of the companies themselves (which, remember, can make money even as you're falling flat on your face), it's most important for you to be hard-nosed and severely practical as you approach each opportunity. Doing so now not only enables you to make the right personal choice but will pay off when you start selling the opportunity to people who will want to know as much as possible before they, too, make the decision to join.

Here's how to go about completing this questionnaire in the right way:

1) Read all the company materials. Then take appropriate information from these materials; use them to answer the questions. **Note:** You'll find when you do this that much of what the companies provide you is not very useful. Companies selling business opportunities are not, in my opinion, very good about providing the kinds of hard information you need to make an informed decision. Indeed, I have never seen a company that provides, in its own printed materials, even half of the information I myself find absolutely necessary to making a considered decision. There's a reason for this.

The executives running most business opportunities are themselves slothful and inefficient. They have never bothered to think through what their prospects really need to know about their companies and so don't bother to provide it. Further, in many cases the information wouldn't read well by prospects. Because so many companies are weak, even outright deceptive, executives consciously suppress important factual information from prospects. Into the often gaping holes left by this process, they are prone to throw in lots of glib adjectives, one unsubstantiated assertion after another, a typhoon of windy rhetoric. The sad thing is that this watered-down presentation works with lots of people, thereby reinforcing in the opportunity executives' minds the feeling that they were right not to provide anything more substantial. People like us, however, demanding wheat and not chaff, are going to help force them to change their operating procedures! Remember what I told you? With the publication of this book, a new day has dawned in network marketing...

2) Grill your upline sponsor. While it is important that you entirely familiarize yourself with the company's materials and glean from them what you can, there's absolutely no reason to do the job all alone. Once you've decided (from your initial conversations with your upline sponsor and from perusing the company's printed materials and listening to their audio cassettes) that this company does hold an initial attraction for you, enlist the further support of your would-be upline sponsor. Mail or fax him a copy of this questionnaire showing the information you've already discovered. Alternatively, go over these questions with him on the phone and fill in the information yourself. Personally, I find it most easy to enter the questions into the computer (where I'll have them both for this review process and for future opportunities) and to work with the upline sponsor over the phone, inputting data as provided. If you do things this way, you can quiz your prospective sponsor on answers that still don't seem very clear to you.

Note: Don't be too surprised if your upline sponsor is pretty unclear about the answers to a good many questions. The probability is that this person didn't bother to do too thorough a vetting of the company before joining and may, despite months or even years in the program, still be unclear on precisely how it works. This lack of clarity doesn't necessarily mean either that the company or sponsor is wrong for you. It just means that you're going to have to be a little more patient and push a little more forcefully to get the information you require.

3) Grill an executive at company headquarters. If your own research and that of your prospective upline sponsor doesn't provide the detailed information you require, go higher — right to company headquarters. It is my firm opinion that *every* business opportunity should have an in-house authority responsible for answering the detailed questions of prospective new distributors. This person should certainly be available during regular business hours and, I submit, beyond. He/she should have one purpose and one purpose only: providing would-be distributors with all the detailed information they need on why this opportunity makes sense for them and exactly how it works. Unfortunately, in my experience very few companies have anything approaching this system. As a result, it is often difficult to know who you should be speaking to and to connect with them in a timely fashion.

Fortunately, your prospective upline sponsor can be of assistance here. This person should call company headquarters and ascertain just who you should be talking to (if he doesn't already know). It may be that this person can supply you with the information you require by answering particular questions on the questionnaire; it may be he will have to talk to you directly. Either way, your prospective sponsor can and should point you in the right direction and smooth the way.

When a company retains my L.A.N.T. System, it's part of the agreement that it will make it easy for both independent distributors and prospects to get in touch with knowledgeable company officials, right to the CEO, to have their questions answered. This is a lot of work, of course; it takes time, dedication and a real commitment to ensuring that people get help and that questions get answered. However, it works. Both distributors and prospects constantly tell me how pleased and grateful they are to be able to have direct access to knowledgeable authorities at the companies and the kind of confidence it gives them. So, let me take a minute here and publicly thank Don Smyth of The Staff of Life, Bill Blaesing & Greg Hilty (co-founders) at Gourmet Coffee Club, and Ed Freeman at The World's Largest Permanent Downline. They are all senior executives... and they all take the time to provide distributors and prospects with just what they need to be able to perform effectively and make intelligent decisions. What you're doing is rare in an industry where chief executive officers customarily hide and where all too many companies make it clear how little providing assistance to distributors counts. Not you guys! You are to be commended for making yourselves available and for your sustained dedication to prospect and distributor success.

Now Look Closely At What You've Discovered

Once you've assembled all this information, scrutinize what you've found. Let me point out several things that are going to mean a lot to you later when you start selling your opportunity:

- **Replicatable Sales Program**

What you absolutely do not want is to be sitting at home trying to figure out how to reinvent the (marketing and recruitment) wheel. You need a complete program from the company, and this program should include:

> ▌ marketing communications (with your name and address on them) that hammer home the most persuasive benefits of joining this company. Unfortunately, you're going to find that most companies keep the presentation focused on themselves, not on the prospect. This is a huge error. Everything any opportunity puts out should be about the prospect; nothing should be about them. On page 7 you see what the cover of a good marketing communication looks like. We call it a self-mailer. Robert and I write them at the National Copywriting Center... Robert Blackman prints them at Diversified Enterprises. They contain the complete "case" for any network marketing company... are inexpensive to buy... and inexpensive to send, going out for just 32 cents.

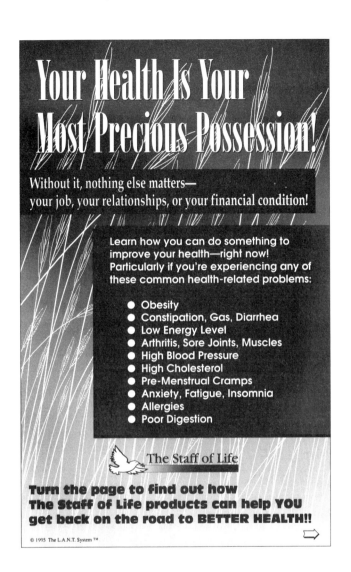

Your Health Is Your Most Precious Possession!

Without it, nothing else matters—
your job, your relationships, or your financial condition!

Learn how you can do something to improve your health—right now! Particularly if you're experiencing any of these common health-related problems:

- Obesity
- Constipation, Gas, Diarrhea
- Low Energy Level
- Arthritis, Sore Joints, Muscles
- High Blood Pressure
- High Cholesterol
- Pre-Menstrual Cramps
- Anxiety, Fatigue, Insomnia
- Allergies
- Poor Digestion

The Staff of Life

Turn the page to find out how The Staff of Life products can help YOU get back on the road to BETTER HEALTH!!

© 1995 The L.A.N.T. System ™

To get several complete self-mailer samples and see for yourself just how handy and convincing they are, send $3 to Robert Blackman, Diversified Enterprises, P.O. Box 1390, Norman, OK 73070. (405) 360-9487.

Robert prints all our self-mailers, and he is expert in producing them.

<Note, each self-mailer is personalized with the name, address, phone and fax of the sender. Does your MLM opportunity offer this service? Or do they gouge you with expensive four-color brochures… and then force you to use a two-bit stamp (that smears) to put your data on?>

▌ a prospect lead-generating program. To succeed with your opportunity you're going to need more and more leads. Does this company provide them to you? Or do they foolishly expect you to generate all your leads yourself? If they do, look elsewhere.

▌ telemarketing support. Does the company assist you by providing scripts and other aids to help you close more people by phone? Or actual hands-on telemarketing support? You want all the help you can get on the phone. Does the opportunity understand this and assist you, or are they too stupid and selfish to get the point?

• The Cost Of The Company's Marketing Communications

I have come to the conclusion that most opportunities are really in the printing business. Why? Take a look at the cost of their glossy four-color brochures and other sales aids. Are they 35 cents? 50 cents? Even a buck each? The actual cost of these is probably a tiny fraction of what the company is charging you; (indeed, if the company orders 100,000 of its four-color brochures at one time they cost about 5 cents!) Thus, the truth is the company is making significant profit selling you their brochures. This is outrageous! An independent-distributor-centered company wants to get as many of its brochures into the hands of its distributor force as possible. They are more worried about assisting the distributor succeed... than gouging the distributors by selling them over-priced "sales aids." Sick, isn't it?

Take a close look at the opportunity you're reviewing. Find out just how expensive the marketing communications are and whether they work... or whether you're just enriching the company by buying them.

• Are You Prohibited From Joining Ad-Net And Other Lead-Generating Programs?

During the writing of this resource, another example of witless network marketing thinking was forcefully brought to my attention. I've got a distributor in Ad-Net, Inc., the lead-generating network marketing program, who also happens to belong to another network marketing company (as all Ad-Net distributors do). The director of marketing at this incredibly stupid company told him that belonging to Ad-Net could be construed as grounds for termination from the company. Why? Because Ad-Net's set-up as a network marketing company!

Now consider just how dumb this comment really is. The first MLM is a company that sells health and nutritional products. Ad-Net is in the business of generating leads for people looking for business opportunities. Anyone with elementary intelligence instantly deduces that the programs are *symbiotic* (the one is product, the other is people to whom to sell the product) — anyone, that is, except for a director of marketing who's so blinkered by avoiding "competition" that she can't tell what's beneficial to distributors and what isn't. So, by whimsical fiat, she waves away something of real value to independent distributors in the field and goes home self-satisfied, feeling sure she's done a good day's work. Ridiculous!

Unless you are one of the privileged few who already has a continuing source of leads, you are going to need all the help you can get generating more leads. You're going to want to use space ads, card-decks, lead-generating programs — and the services of companies like Ad-Net, Inc. Personally, I prefer Ad-Net to its competitors because Ad-Net generates most of its leads directly from ads; the other companies use mailing lists, where people are not necessarily looking for an opportunity and haven't asked for any information. In practice, this makes them very poor prospects.

But whatever program you select, you've got to be sure some idiot at corporate headquarters isn't going to terminate you because you're using perfectly legitimate ways to generate leads. Yet, in the often hilariously short-sighted world of MLM, this is what happens. Take my word for it: it's a mistake to become affiliated with any company that won't let you get all the leads you can, in all the ways you can. Case closed.

• *The Company Compensation Plan*

Know precisely how you make money in this opportunity. Review both ostensible and hidden fees, that is any monthly or other dues and the additional cost of using particular services. Find out precisely when your compensation will be paid... and talk to a couple of other distributors to find out if the company meets its obligations in a timely fashion. Your prospects are going to want to know about the money, believe me, so the more you find out here the more persuasive and solid your presentation is going to be.

• *Five Most Persuasive Reasons For Joining The Company*

All opportunities should focus on just three things:

A) keeping their competitive advantage;

B) making sure the company is well managed, that routine business is handled expeditiously, and that all those who have legitimate reason for approaching the company find that their business is efficiently taken care of;

C) marketing their competitive advantage in an unrelenting fashion, that is using this competitive advantage to generate the maximum number of prospect leads and closing the maximum number of prospect leads.

Reviewing these three crucial aspects of business success, you can immediately see just how important competitive advantage is. To this end, it's crucial that you understand and use the five most persuasive reasons for joining the company. Let me show you what I mean.

Here, for instance, are the kinds of persuasive reasons we use with our Staff of Life, Gourmet Coffee and Ad-Net opportunities:

1) these companies offer products that people are already using or should be using because of their existing interests. In other words, we are not so much trying to change people's habits, as make use of those habits. There are, for instance, 100,000,000+ American coffee drinkers, (hence the desirability of Gourmet Coffee). Tens of millions are taking responsibility for their health and wish to get into a sensible health regime; (thus the benefit of The Staff of Life). And all network marketers need a continual supply of prospect leads; (hence the need for Ad-Net).

2) Since you're going to use these products anyway, buy them from yourself. One of the key marketing points of what we do is a very simple principle. Don't just buy products. Buy the products/services you need... but get more than the products/services themselves. Here's what I mean. If you go to a grocery story, you can buy coffee. That's fine but there's only one benefit involved: you get coffee. If, however, you buy coffee from Gourmet Coffee Club you not only get the coffee itself (benefit #1), you can do what's necessary to get it for free (namely recruit 12 people on the Standing Order Plan) (benefit #2), and you can develop a useful additional income source (benefit #3). You cannot get benefits 2 and 3 if you purchase coffee in a store — which is a very persuasive reason for joining.

3) you get a total marketing system. The problem for most people in MLM is that it's too complicated for them. Because of the parent company's laxness and lack of constructive support, independent distributors are asked to become trained marketers and develop an entire system. That's not true with our companies. We conceive and develop a complete marketing package. We generate prospect leads, provide detailed guidelines for closing them, provide equally detailed guidelines for maintaining ongoing relations and showing how to get them to purchase products, recruit, *etc*. We provide telemarketing support... advertising support... and ongoing marketing support through the company publications.

4) an essential element of this system is inexpensive, client-centered marketing communications. Whereas in most MLM companies, you are coerced into buying many different kinds of expensive marketing communications, our belief is different. With us, you get company-approved marketing communications that you can personalize with your name, address, phone, fax and company i.d. These communications contain everything a prospect needs to know about the company, include a direct access number to company personnel who make themselves available to answer questions, and provide both sign-up and product order forms. In short, one-stop shopping!

5) you get additional team marketing support. We operate as a giant, international team. The problem with most upline sponsors is that they recruit you and abandon you. Not us. Day 1 you receive detailed instructions from both Dr. Jeffrey Lant and Robert Blackman (separately) on how to make your involvement a success. Both make themselves available for constructive consultations with team members (which means these team members must be doing their homework and implementing the system to make these consultations productive). And a team newsletter with additional marketing suggestions is regularly produced. In short, there is *team* support, wherever you fall in the Lant/Blackman organization.

Take a close look at these benefits. These present benefits both of interest to the consumer (get fine, useful products and get them for free) and for the entrepreneur (look at the system you get for developing increasing monthly income). Both are important.

I'd venture to guess that in any MLM organization fully 80% of the people will not become entrepreneurs. They'll dabble, of course, now and then recruiting someone, but they usually get in to enjoy the products. That's fine, if that's all they want to do. You've got to be prepared for them. Thus, stress the consumer benefits they get (how good the coffee is, how valuable the health products with the kinds of benefits they deliver). For the other 20%, the crucial entrepreneurs, you need to stress duplicatable system. They want to know that they're getting into something that works, something that will grow if they pursue the system properly. Convince them! Once an entrepreneur is making money in your opportunity, he/she is in for the duration, and that means more money every month for you!

Unfortunately, when you review the marketing communications of most MLM companies you find they don't do what's necessary to make consumers feel good about getting in, providing the benefits they need... and they certainly don't provide smart entrepreneurs with what *they* need to know, namely that the company offers a complete recruiting system. These, of course, are companies to avoid.

How You're Probably Feeling About Now

 When you've finished gathering all the necessary information, tabulating it, comparing it, really analyzing it, you may not only be a little worn out, you're probably going to be a little discouraged. Why, so much of what you've reviewed is fluff, so many companies entirely unprepared for the serious business of building a field force of independent distributors, thinking through what these distributors need and working hard to provide it to them. You may well be wondering if there are any good, solid, distributor-centered opportunities in the land. Well, friend, the answer is damned few.

But let me tell you something else: it's a lot better that you find this out in the comfort of your home or office, after your professional search, after the investment of just a little money and just a little time, instead of a couple of months into the exercise when you've discovered all this by sad experience.

The fact is, most "opportunities" aren't opportunities at all; they're bottomless pits. Every day I am contacted by people who have discovered that the people who run opportunities of every kind are not focused on honing their competitive advantage, perfecting their internal management, and are certainly not focused on doing everything possible to assist their independent distributors succeed. Inevitably, such a discovery is disheartening for you... just as it was for me.

When I found this sad state of affairs to be the norm, not the exception, in the hyperbole-filled opportunity industry, I found myself at the crossroads you, too, may now be facing. And I took the road of deciding to do something about it.

See the next page to find out what...

CHAPTER 2

THE L.A.N.T. SYSTEM™ — LUCRATIVE ADVANCEMENTS IN NETWORKING TACTICS

If, after your research, you find a company that is well run, with manageable debt and solid management, a company that has worked hard on developing superior products and honing its competitive position, but which does not support its independent distributor field force in the ways outlined above, you have a decision to make. You can either

> 1) abandon the company and keep on looking for a more perfect situation; (See Appendix IV, page 141 for ideas.)
>
> 2) use the company's marketing communications and system, even though they are weak (which usually produces failure and lots of unnecessary frustration and wasted resources), or
>
> 3) you can turn to The L.A.N.T. SYSTEM™ and hitch my marketing engine to your opportunity.

The L.A.N.T. SYSTEM™ stands for "Lucrative Advancements in Networking Tactics." It is the result of prolonged observation and analysis of many hundreds of network marketing and other opportunities. My rescarch yielded the finding that opportunity executives focus on

- product first
- management second, and
- independent distributors a very distant third, if at all.

Upon reflection it is easy to see why this is so:

- Product is the easiest problem to deal with. All that one needs to do is review existing products/services in any given field and so arrange matters that the product the company is offering is superior in any number of ways. While this may take a certain amount of technical dexterity and intelligence, it is not otherwise difficult.

- Management is alluring because it involves the receipt and disbursement of money, and money is the real reason why people go through all the headaches of starting and operating opportunities. Naturally good management of any opportunity is absolutely necessary but a focus on internal management to the exclusion of the processes that produce the money in the first place just doesn't make sense.

- Distributor development is, by comparison, more difficult. It demands that a company turn its attention from its own products and the ever exciting world of intra-office politics and games-playing to the more taxing and time-consuming world of people development. Ultimately, a company must not only be willing to build a completely replicatable recruiting program... but to spend time ensuring that all the distributors who are brought in are taught to use it profitably. This is entirely do-able, of course, but it can be tedious and time-consuming. It's so much more fun to gossip about company personnel and day-dream about the big bucks coming down the pike than spend yet another hour with long-winded Mrs. McGillicutty, a small-time distributor from Kansas City. Yet it must never be forgotten... it is the Mrs. McGillicuttys numbering in their thousands who produce the big bucks for the company. NEVER FORGET THIS!!! Thus, attending to their welfare is crucial.

Enter The L.A.N.T. SYSTEM[TM]

I created The L.A.N.T. SYSTEM[TM] out of necessity when I saw that opportunity executives had completely missed the boat on independent distributor development. And I mean completely. They were willing to do anything — add another staff member, add another four-color brochure, hype up all their pronouncements — rather than face the obvious fact that in an opportunity that relies on independent distributors, supporting these independent distributors is more than a priority; it's the future of the company.

Failure to recognize this fact has been one of the major reasons why the large majority of opportunities fail. Because they don't focus on developing the independent distributor and ensuring the rivulets of money these distributors regularly ship to headquarters, the companies themselves all too quickly atrophy and die.

But with The L.A.N.T. SYSTEM[TM] *this needn't happen.*

In the L.A.N.T. SYSTEM[TM] the independent distributor is fully supported, which constitutes its primary reason for being. Each independent distributor gets:

- step-by-step instructions on how to sponsor and maintain his/her organization;

- self-mailer marketing communications (both hard-copy and on diskette) that allow the company to both control its case and make it in the most effective way. Each self-mailer contains all the essential reasons about why the company's product line is superior and business opportunity profitable. Self-mailers are inexpensive to produce and inexpensive to send. Indeed, they are sent for just the cost of the basic first-class stamp.

- as many prospect leads as he/she wants. No organization can grow unless all members have prospect leads. Getting these leads into the hands of each distributor is a prime reason for the L.A.N.T. SYSTEM™ existing — and its success.

- telemarketing support. This telemarketing support, provided by a company called Tele-Close, came into existence because I was continually told by distributors either that they had no time to make calls... or didn't feel comfortable doing so. Now these problems are solved. Professional telemarketers are available to make all prospect calls for any distributor.

What's more, because no system that deals with people and their changing needs can afford to remain static, the L.A.N.T. SYSTEM™ (as provided to companies) offers on-going marketing consultation both to the company and to independent distributors through marketing tips offered in the company's newsletter, to the company CEO, *etc.*

In short, the L.A.N.T. SYSTEM™ does precisely what no company in the entire network marketing industry has ever done: focuses squarely on the independent distributor and offers each distributor a completely replicatable system expressly designed (and regularly improved) to enhance distributor success. So sensible, it constantly astonishes me that no one else in an industry supposedly involving millions ever bothered either to think through the problem... or to do what was necessary to solve it. But, in the best American tradition, I have found the need and filled it... to the inexpressible delight of independent distributors nationwide — and now you! Let's take a look at the major component of the L.A.N.T. SYSTEM™.

The L.A.N.T. SYSTEM™ is divided into three main parts:

▮ client-centered marketing communications

▮ regular lead-generating programs, and

▮ telemarketing support.

Client-Centered Marketing Communications

When you look at the marketing communications produced by most opportunities, you understand just how little their executives know about marketing. All marketing communications should be based on just four simple words:

YOU GET BENEFIT NOW

The "you" in this sentence is the person the marketing communication is intended for. In the opportunity market there are just two important people: the independent distributor who needs help selling the opportunity... and the prospect who is being recruited. Thus, there are only two kinds of marketing communications that need to be created for opportunities:

> i) the communications that provide the distributor with clear guidelines and details on what to do to sell the opportunity, and

> ii) the communications that provide the prospect with the benefit information he needs about the opportunity and motivates him to join it.

All other communications are superfluous and wasteful of resources.

The word "get" is key because that's what an opportunity is all about — *getting something*. Again, there are only two people for whom this is relevant — the independent distributor... and the prospect.

And what do they get? *BENEFITS*. I've written a lot over the years about benefits and how they differ from features, but it never hurts to hit this vital point yet again. A feature is an *aspect* of something... like a 60-minute audio cassette about your opportunity. Features have color, size, weight, certain dimensions, defined elements. Featured are necessarily centered on the thing itself.

Benefits, by comparison, are about the person you're talking to in your marketing communication. If the feature is a 60-minute audio cassette, the benefit is being provided with 15 low-cost things you can do right now to generate prospects who will be interested in buying your opportunity. See the difference? A handy way of differentiating between features and benefits is to remember that lines about features begin "it is" or "it has" while benefit lines start "You get..."

The final crucial word, of course, is NOW! — the only moment in marketing that matters. Marketing communications are correct when they get the person being spoken to to take immediate action. Not action tomorrow or action next week. ACTION NOW! Marketing communications fail — no matter how much color is used, what kinds of papers and inks and elaborate design — if they do not motivate immediate action; they succeed when such immediate action is motivated.

NOW!

By this token, then, the marketing communications sold by the vast majority of network marketing communications are a complete waste of time and resources. They are clearly not focused on the all-important "you"... don't talk about what that person gets... haven't bothered to translate features into benefits... even if they present features at all... and certainly don't do what it takes to motivate people to take immediate action NOW!

Don't just take my word for this either. While you're doing your research into which network marketing opportunity to support, you're going to get your mitts on lots and lots of marketing communications. Marketers from Maine to California will have spent lots of their time and the company's money to produce these babies... and yet the lot is sadly deficient, mere exercises in egotistical self-glorification rather than doing what marketing communications are supposed to do: motivate people to move.

I deal with this problem through my National Copywriting Center. Here Robert Blackman and I and our copywriting associates specialize in producing client-centered "cash copy"... that is copy based on the four essential little words above. This copy, of course, is the essence of all marketing communications including cover letters, brochures, ads, flyers, and post cards. But we've added our own unique wrinkle: self-mailers.

As you've already seen from the example provided, our self-mailers are entirely self-contained sales packages that:

- deliver all the client-centered benefits in one document;

- are personalized with your name, address, phone, fax and company i.d. numbers;

- contain your company applications ready for the prospect to complete, and

- are mailed for the cost of a first-class stamp (now 32 cents).

As anyone knows who has been in network marketing more than an hour, all network marketing companies produce a plethora of marketing communications; more, when recruiting is down or they just have nothing better to do around headquarters, their invariable solution to recruiting problems is to produce another. This may make sense from their standpoint (remember, all opportunities are in the printing business and make a substantial amount of their revenue selling marketing communications to the unsuspecting independent distributor)... but it makes no sense from yours.

What YOU need is not sixteen different marketing communications that aren't client-centered and don't fit together to make a convincing case. You need ONE marketing communication that provides the prospect with the absolutely crucial benefit information he needs about the company... and motivates him to sign the application form that's in the communication right this minute.

Resource

Let my National Copywriting Center assist you and your company produce self-mailers and other marketing communications, call me at (617) 547-6372.

Note: even if you (mistakenly) decide not to produce your own self-mailers, we can still help. Once you join my Ad-Net, Inc. organization, you can use our very popular Ad-Net self-mailers in conjunction with any other marketing communications you may be using. You'll find them a very handy way to develop your Ad-Net organization! You get these self-mailers from Robert Blackman.

Regular Lead-Generating Programs

Last night I participated in a telephone conference call with another one of the innumerable nit-wits who thinks he's a network marketing expert... but hasn't a clue about what network marketing is all about and how to make it work. This time the discussion focused on one of the lead-generating programs I recommend, in this case Ad-Net, and whether working it would divert this fellow's distributors from focusing on their main opportunity. I quizzed the man...

- Does your opportunity provide its independent distributors/your people with a regular source of leads? No!

- Do any of your distributors have a regular source of leads because of another business, *etc.*? No!

- Do you generate leads for your people and make them available at regular intervals? No!

- Do you think a regular source of leads for yourself and all your distributors would be helpful? Well, I'm not really sure. I mean, shouldn't the distributor be focusing on just one program?

- <Do you have a brain in your head or are you one of the legion of witless fools in network marketing who thinks your products sell themselves?>...

I didn't ask the last question, but I should have. Here's a man wondering whether working Ad-Net to bring his people a regular supply of leads would divert them when he has ensured that his people will have no leads whatsoever to work.

Then he asked me, "If Ad-Net's so good, why haven't the 'leaders' in my company recommended it to me?"

God help me, I had the greatest difficulty in not laughing aloud and calling down the very saints to see this fool in the flesh...

"Sir," I said, "your 'leaders' have created a system that ensures that neither you nor your people have a regular lead flow... and you ask me why they haven't recommended this to you. I suggest you seek other leaders."

(By the way, when I asked this fellow how long he'd been working his opportunity and how many active distributors he had, his answer was hardly surprising — three years and just thirty. How could it be otherwise when the necessary fertilizer of prospect leads was missing? The plant was starving for lack of nutrient.)

Opportunities work in large part because each independent distributor (you!) does EVERYTHING POSSIBLE to generate the maximum number of leads and to direct them with the utmost speed into the hands of people in his organization to work them. The exercise goes something like this:

- you get recruited. You immediately launch as many lead-generating projects as possible.

- as leads come in, you use them to recruit at least ONE person ASAP. You get this person to immediately launch as many lead-generating projects as possible. In the short-term, you may either share some of your own leads with this recruit... and/or charge him a certain sum in order to enlarge your own lead-generating projects which will, in due course, provide him with at least a percentage of the leads he needs.

- the person you have recruited uses these leads to recruit at least one person... and then follows the directions to get him to start generating leads... and may lend/sell or otherwise provide this person with sufficient leads so he can recruit another person ASAP.

As soon as you've assisted your first recruit to get started with enough leads... you prime your lead-generating pump (producing more leads) so that you are ready to do the SAME THING when your next crop of leads produces your next recruit, *etc*.

Thus, recruit one person... distribute leads to this recruit so he can recruit one... stimulate lead-producing mechanisms to produce more leads from which you recruit your second person... distributing leads to this recruit so he can recruit someone else... *etc*.

Or, think of it like this: RECRUIT ACROSS, DISTRIBUTE LEADS DOWN, RE-CRUIT ACROSS AGAIN, DISTRIBUTE LEADS DOWN AGAIN, *ETC*.

This is not, of course, at all the way network marketing and other opportunities currently work. In these characteristic situations you are recruited... you are told to focus on your "warm market" (namely family, friends, co-workers, associates, *etc*.)... then you are abandoned, to sink or swim as the fates (and your own talents) allow. Of course, the vast majority of people sink. They run through their warm markets lickety split, inevitably making a few sales (after all, Aunt Sally has always supported you) but failing to do what's absolutely crucial to building a business, namely securing permanent and regular prospect lead supplies.

The L.A.N.T. SYSTEM^{TM} To The Rescue

The L.A.N.T. SYSTEM™ starts from the proposition that it is wrong and indeed iniquitous to get friends, family and co-workers involved in your projects unless and until you have done everything possible in other ways to secure the prosperity of your opportunity. If you opened a restaurant you might well tell your friends and relatives you were doing so... but you wouldn't base the prosperity and future of your enterprise on whether these people used your service. No, indeed, you'd be out and about hustling for customers. It is precisely this "out and about" stuff (called lead-generating) with which the opportunity companies short-sightedly and stupidly fail to assist you.

If you are going to make your opportunity a success, you must become an expert in lead-generating. You must be willing to start small and, as your organization grows, do everything possible to increase the number of lead-generating outlets and work them to ensure they generate the maximum number of leads which you can then distribute throughout your organization. If you are not willing to do this you have ensured your own failure... and that of all the people you have so laboriously sponsored.

CHAPTER 3

GENERATING ALL THE LEADS YOU AND YOUR DOWNLINE NEED

Lead-generating vehicles with which you must become familiar include:

- space ads
- card-decks and lead-generating "bingo" cards
- companies which generate leads.

Let's review each.

Space Ads

If you're going to be a success recruiting, you've got to work with the most highly qualified leads. The process of securing these leads — and hence the ultimate close you must have — starts with the copy you use in marketing communications such as space ads.

Take a look at the ads below, ads I'm currently using for Gourmet Coffee Club and The Staff of Life.

These ads work because they're:

- focused on the prospects we're trying to attract. In the case of the Gourmet Coffee Club that's coffee drinkers (remember there are over 100,000,000 American coffee drinkers alone), and only secondarily on business opportunity seekers. In the case of The Staff of Life, that's people with the kinds of listed conditions that Staff of Life products can help with.

- packed with believable benefits and not hype. Hype may attract responses, but always the wrong responses. You want the same kind of people we want: people who are looking for credible value.

- about products that people will not just buy once, but keep on buying over and over, month after month. What would you rather have, a one-time sale, or a lifetime sale?

- offering a good reason for immediate action — not just "free information" but a free 20-page report that provides more information on what the prospect is really interested in.

Running space ads is on very sensible way of getting leads. Yet very few people in MLM have a space ad plan. This is ridiculous.

Such a plan must include:

- writing a variety of client-centered ads. These ads must be focused on generating the maximum number of qualified responses nationwide. (By the way, as I wrote this section at 7 a.m. a prospect called in. Yes, 7 a.m. You must be prepared for such action AT ALL TIMES. When ads are good, your prospects will call round the clock. Be advised!)

Note: It goes without saying that writing these kinds of ads is one of the primary functions of the National Copywriting Center cited above. If you want such ads to provide prospects for yourself and your organization, call me.

- joining Ad-Net. One of the benefits of membership in Ad-Net is that each month the company sends you a certificate which you can use as payment for free space-ad advertising. Here's what the certificate looks like.

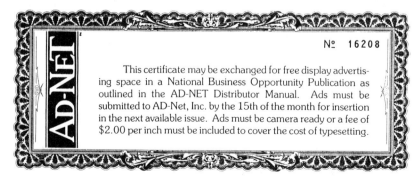

- creating space-ad co-ops. Remember, you need as many leads as you can get. The way to ensure that you get at least some of them is to keep organizing space-ad co-ops. After you join Ad-Net this is both necessary and easy. To be effective a co-op needs camera-ready ad copy, an organizer who will gather the necessary certificates and place the ads, and a system for dispersing the prospect leads once they're generated. For this system to work you need:

■ a sheet with co-op operating directions, (remember, you're going to keep having to remind people how your system works);

■ a letter or memo which reminds people in your organization to keep submitting certificates;

■ a convenient place to keep certificates;

■ a standard form letter to use when submitting certificates either to Ad-Net or to an ad placement representative;

■ a standard letter which you'll use for dispatching information to distributors on prospect leads who telephoned in response to the ad;

■ a standard letter which you'll use for dispatching leads mailed in.

Let's take a look at each of these necessary elements.

■ Sheet With Co-Op Operating Directions

Keep in mind, when you join an opportunity you are creating a business, and all businesses need completely replicatable procedures. The objective is to think through what you need, create it, and then have it available in convenient form (on computer whenever possible) for use and reuse. In this connection, write down the operating directions for your space-ad co-op. These directions should include:

- the name of the person organizing the co-op
- his/her address/phone/fax
- where you want certificates sent (if different from above)
- when you want certificates sent (the correct response here is "the minute you receive them")
- day of the month you send in the certificates to Ad-Net or the agent (it's best to send them in just once a month and to let people in your organization know when that is)
- how long it takes for people participating in the co-op to get responses (they always want to know)

- kinds of publications (the specific names if you know them) where the ads will run (people like to know this and look out for them)

- how leads are dispersed once people respond

- how and when to call if there are questions (personally, I prefer these kinds of calls in the evening whenever possible).

▌ Reminder Memo

Don't think you can simply tell people in your downline once that they should submit their certificates each month and that that's an end to the matter. No way. The one month I forgot to put this information in my monthly downline newsletter was, predictably, the one month when we received the fewest certificates. Whether you like it or not, you're going to have to keep reminding people in your organization to send in their certificates. Thus, you need a reminder memo.

This memo, of course, can and should be short. A paragraph will do. Something like this:

MAIL IN YOUR CERTIFICATES FOR THE SPACE AD CO-OP

Make sure to send me your Ad-Net certificates each month by (date) so you can participate in our space-ad co-op lead-generating program. Don't wait to the last minute to get your certificates in. Send them to me THE DAY YOU RECEIVE THEM. You will receive leads from any given certificate about 60 days after you've sent it in.

Send your certificate to /your name, address/.

If questions, call /your telephone number/.

Something as simple as this will do nicely. Sent it out about two weeks before your deadline.

▌ Convenient Place To Store Certificates

Even if you use an old shoebox, make sure you've got one place where you put all your Ad-Net free ad certificates. When they come in from members of your downline, check to ensure that the person's name and address are on the back of each certificate. If not, write them in yourself. Then deposit them immediately in the safe place from whence you can draw them out again when you're ready to submit them.

▌ Standard Submission Form Letter

Remember, the object of business is to make all actions as efficient as possible, especially routine actions. To this end, since you're going to be sending in free ad certificates monthly, develop a standard form letter for doing so as soon as possible.

If you're going to submit the certificates directly to Ad-Net, call the company to see who (at any given moment) is handling the certificates. Contact this person to check current procedures. Then incorporate these procedures and the name of the responsible Ad-Net employee into your letter, thus:

Dear /Ad-Net employee handling the free certificate program/,

Enclosed please find /number of/ certificates from members of my organization and camera-ready art.

Please run this art in /name of publication/s/ as soon as possible. Have the publication send me a checking copy whenever possible.

If you have any questions about this matter, contact me directly at /your phone/.

Note: this same letter can be used when submitting certificates to your ad placement representative.

▌ Standard Letter For Dispatching Information To Distributors On Phoned-In Prospect Leads

Prospect leads arrive in two major ways: by telephone and by mail. You need standard form letters for each.

When the lead arrives by phone it's, by definition, a presumably higher quality lead than the people who just mail in the lead. Why? Because it costs more to make the phone call and because the person reckons you are going to do some pre-qualifying right away. Which you jolly well should!

Ask the caller questions like these:

- Have you ever been in network marketing?
- Have you been successful?
- If so, to what extent?
- Are you actively seeking a business opportunity now?
- Are you looking at other opportunities? If so, which ones?
- What kinds of things are you particularly looking for in an opportunity?
- Do you have at least 5 hours a week to work an opportunity?
- Do you have at least /whatever you've determined is the basic budget to work the opportunity/?
- Will you be willing to read our material? Will you talk to me and others to make sure you really understand what makes our opportunity so good?

If the prospect passes this necessary pre-qualifying quiz, you've got a superbly qualified lead on your hand. You need to get it into the hands of one of your distributors ASAP, by fax if at all possible. The communication in which you dispatch this information should say:

From: you

To: lucky distributor getting this prospect lead

The following has just called in response to an ad. I have determined through pre-qualifying questions that this person has high interest in our opportunity; /change this phrase if necessary based on what you've discovered during your questioning/. This prospect knows that you'll be sending company information and following up.

prospect name

address

day ph

eve ph

fax

(Add any additional comments about this person that you've discovered or deem relevant to the closing process.)

P.S. Report back to me at your earliest convenience and let me know if you've been able to close this lead.

Now fax this information immediately.

Note: One of the things that consistently amazes and delights people considering membership in one of my élite Success Teams is the speed with which their query is followed up. But, frankly, there's no mystery about this. It's a matter of judgment.

If the prospect indicates to me that he/she is very interested, the lead is handled accordingly. The prospect data goes to one of the best people I've got in the area where the prospect lives/works. I urge my representative to take appropriately prompt action and then follow up to close. If my representative stumbles by procrastinating or failing to follow through (as occasionally happens), you can believe me when I say they get some Trumanesque hell from me. And if it happens again, my assistance in generating leads for them stops. In this business, only the good deserve to be helped.

Note: if you can't fax the phoned in lead data to your team members, don't worry. You can either call in the lead data and give it directly to your distributor or leave it on an answering machine, confirming by mail. This will do almost as well as a fax.

∎ Standard Letter For Dispatching Information To Your Downline On Mailed-In Prospect Leads

Mailed-in leads may not need quite the white-hot response of phoned-in leads, but you've got to move promptly with them, too. In practice this means that all leads mailed to you should be re-mailed to your distributors WITHIN 24 HOURS. If you're like me, you'll get your mailed-in leads in the morning and can have them sorted and out in the afternoon mail. I pride myself on this and so should you. But what helps is having a form letter to expedite the matter. In this letter

- point out the importance of working these leads right away — the day they receive them whenever possible;

- make sure your distributor gets on the phone to qualify these leads. This means talking to prospects right away and finding out if they are really looking for an opportunity, will read what the distributor sends and listen to his/her message. (Use the questions I provided above as a guide.) If not, this person is not a real prospect and should be removed from consideration. If on the other hand, the person emerges as a strong prospect, more attention can and should be provided.

- you should provide follow-up guidelines. The prospect is not always (or even usually) going to be available for the first qualifying call. Ditto the first closing call. You must ask your distributors to persist. It astonishes me that so many distributors expect everything to fall into place in their budding businesses with a single letter, a single phone call. Get real! The business of building a business is difficult and time-consuming. Connecting with people, providing information to people, motivating people, persuading people all take time. If your distributors don't know this, it's your responsibility to tell them!

- list common objections your distributor will hear and provide your advice for answering them. (One of the good things about the L.A.N.T. SYSTEM™ is that each distributor receives a list of common objections to either purchasing product from the company or joining the opportunity... and the right way to respond to them. You should provide this, too!)

- remind your distributors of the five key reasons for joining your opportunity. Don't assume that they know them... and don't make the mistake of providing these reasons only once. Keep hitting your distributors with these reasons over and over again until they can recite them in their sleep! Remember, you must constantly re-mail this information to your distributors. It's a drag... but it's absolutely necessary.

My main point here is: don't just send leads. Send a lead-closing *system*. One of the main things I've discovered in building my own network marketing organizations is that I have to do the thinking. My job is to brainstorm options, pick the best ones, create the necessary materials and provide them to my downline. Yes, I *think*. I ask of my downline only that they *execute* and report back to me on their findings. If what I'm creating works, we continue it. If it doesn't, it's back to the drawing board! This means that in *each* organization, ideally in *each* MLM central office, there must be one master planner... and lots of people willing to closely follow directions. Unfortunately, in reality, in most companies there is NO master planner and lots of people in the field moving aimlessly, some trying to find a way that works, the majority giving up right away. What an idiotic situation!

Resource

As your organization (and its Ad-Net counterpart) grows, you'll want and need your space ads in more and more publications. Remember, a growing business can NEVER have too many prospect leads, and it is your job to keep expanding your lead-producing capacity. When you stop doing this, your organization will atrophy and die. To build capacity for space-ad lead-generation, I suggest you contact sooner rather than later my friend Dr. Robert Davidson. Davidson is a remarkable fellow who has two very full careers. On the one hand he's a veterinarian with an active practice. On the other hand, he runs a variety of publications and places ads in hundreds more. Write and ask him for a copy of his publication "Discount Advertising." It shows you how you can get discount advertising in newspapers, magazines, card deck and on radio. Contact him at Interstate Enterprises, P.O. Drawer 19689, Houston, TX 77224. Once your camera-ready ads are available, send them to Davidson to keep on file. Then have the person who's collecting Ad-Net certificates for you send them all in to him once a month. Davidson will place the ads (if there are particular places where you'd like them, you may say so) and send you confirmations. The publications will send tear sheets for your files. As your Ad-Net organization grows, you'll have more and more certificates to submit to Davidson and, in due course, lots more leads to distribute. Make sure to include your phone number in the ad so you can qualify people who phone in, as per my instructions.

Note: If your company retains The L.A.N.T. SYSTEM™, we'll automatically create camera-ready ads for your opportunity. These will automatically be approved by the company. All Ad-Net certificates will be sent direct to the company which will deal directly with Davidson. Responses to the ads will come back to the company and they'll distribute them to participants.

Another note: if you're organizing co-ops where people pay for participating in them instead of using certificates, fine. Just follow the procedures above, substituting "cash" for "certificates." You'll find yourself organizing lots of co-ops in this way, so it's good to get your procedures down ASAP.

Card-Decks And Lead-Generating Bingo Cards

Again, I must stress: when you go into any business opportunity and really want to prosper, you must understand all the lead-generating mechanisms available to you. This means exploration, experimentation, and analysis.

One of the ways you're certainly going to want to use is card-decks, both for full cards on your opportunity and for the shorter ads which appear on lead-generating "bingo cards."

You probably already know what a card deck is: a package of 3" x 5" post cards packed in cellophane and mailed together to a targeted group of prospects. However, if you've never seen one, be sure to write or call me; I'll be happy to send you a sample.

You see, I've been a card-deck publisher for many years now. I started my card-deck on the proverbial kitchen table. Such humble surroundings, however, gave me a real advantage in the deck business: incredibly low overhead. I knew that if I 1) lowered the retail price to rock bottom, and 2) retained high printing and high list quality, I'd have 3) a very profitable business. And so it has proved. While my competitors kept their prices unrealistically high (most charge two or even three times as much as I do for the same circulation), I charged (and have continued to charge) the lowest prices in the industry... and, in short order, built the largest card-deck in America. My customers get high-quality printing, top-quality lists, on-time mailing, free second color, *and* the lowest prices. I make money — and get to experiment with lots of cards promoting my products and services, including my network marketing opportunities. Fair trade.

In this process, I have learned a lot about how to use card-decks to promote a network marketing opportunity, and I'd like to share these insights with you now.

- Resolve to use card-decks. There isn't another print medium in the world that produces leads as fast as card-decks do. Just a few days after mailing, your card will "hit." After it does, look out. Businesses that customarily get just a few leads in a day may, all of a sudden, get many dozens or even hundreds of leads. This is hardly surprising since opportunity cards are popular and draw well. With the kind of client-centered card that our National Copywriting Center copywriters regularly turn out, you can expect anywhere between 1/2 of one percent response (500) up to 1 and 1/2 per cent response (1500). Face it. This is a lot of people to have to deal with.

- Resolve not to pay to be in card-decks. Reread this line. Smart people running opportunities benefit from card-decks without putting in anything more than a little sweat equity. How's this? Easy... The power of network marketing lies in its leveraging potential... in recruiting other people who will, in effect, be working for you (at the same time they're working for themselves). Card-decks are the perfect fuel for network marketing success, especially when you appoint yourself Card-Deck Organizer-in-Chief. In my deck, 100,000 two-color cards currently cost $1399. To get your leads for free (and have others use *their* money to build *your* organization) all you need to do is get each of 14 people to pay you $100 and the card is paid for. At this point, I recommend you divide all incoming leads into 15 shares; (the extra one is for you, to compensate you for being so bright and your willingness to organize the co-op). All the other leads are distributed to the people paying for them.

Consider the benefits of organizing a co-op:

1) at least 14 people in your organization are supplied with leads that they'll be working on their behalf — and on *yours*;

2) you can request of the card-deck publisher that he refrain from publishing a card from anyone else associated with the company you're promoting; (publishers are generally sensitive to your need for exclusivity in your company). You thereby block your internal competitors from using this medium against you.

3) you get *free* leads for yourself.

Now, consider this. At any given time there are about 10 card-decks (running between 3-6 times a year each) that are appropriate for running an opportunity card. (For a complete list, check out *Standard Rate and Data* in your library or write SRDS Publishing, 3004 Glenview Road, Wilmette, IL 60091.) As your organization grows, you'll be like the kudzu vine, quickly expanding into each. This, of course, is precisely what you want. Your objective is to take over *all* decks... and to have your organization purchasing shares for *each*... and getting you *free* leads from *each*.

It's clear to me now that very few people in network marketing understand this concept. Astonishing numbers of independent distributors approach MLM as if it were an old-fashioned country store, where you have to serve people one at a time. Indeed, I'm thinking now of a woman I know working a particular network marketing opportunity. Her understanding has so progressed that she at least runs cards in card decks. That, at least, is to the good. But she still doesn't understand that she herself should be working only a tiny portion of the leads her cards draw. Instead, she runs cards... gets a high response... and then runs herself ragged attempting to work all the leads herself. THIS WOMAN MUST BE CRAZY. WORSE, SHE MUST BE STUPID, SINCE SHE REFUSES TO LEARN HOW TO USE THE TOOLS OF HER CHOSEN TRADE.

The correct way of handling the situation is like this:

Let's say you decide to use card-decks from Day 1 of your involvement in network marketing, a day when you have absolutely no one in your organization and no great prospects. No problem. Everyone's got to start somewhere.

- First, find out how few cards you can buy from any given card-deck. Most decks will, if pressed, offer to sell you half a run (called a "split run"). Unlike other decks, however, I actually advertise this service and make it freely available. 50,000 cards in one of my decks cost just $750. For this investment you'll still get the .5%-1.5% return mentioned above.

- Since you have no people in your organization to co-op with, you must either 1) decide to work all the leads yourself, or 2) attempt to form a co-op with your upline sponsor. I suggest the latter. Your upline sponsor is, after all, more knowledgeable about the program than you are; moreover, he can attempt to sell response shares to people in his organization... who are not in your organization. In other words, he can become an active partner in the sale and dispersal of the responses.

But what if this person is as poor and myopic as most upline sponsors are, making excuses instead of getting on with the job? (By the way, when you hear excuses like — "I'm want to work my 'warm market' instead", or "I don't want to work any leads outside the neighborhood", you know your upline is not the kind of person you should have affiliated with. Run, don't walk, to another connection.) In this case, escalate to *his* upline... and so on until you've either exhausted your possibilities (discerning in the process lots of clues about the people you've decided to work with and the company that attracts such drones)... or found a kindred spirit who really wants to build a national business that generates big revenue for you both.

If you can't find a kindred spirit and you've decided to stick with this company and these people... go ahead and purchase at least 50,000 cards for yourself. But when you do, make a resolution. Resolve that this is the first and only time you'll do this. Resolve that you'll do what's necessary (namely recruit kindred spirits) so that next time you'll get at least 50,000 cards *without* having to pay for them!!! Now, get on with the job at hand.

• Having committed for the space, do what's necessary to stimulate the greatest possible response... and handle it expeditiously.

As far as generating the greatest response is concerned:

1) create a client-centered card. This card should focus on all the benefits of your program. What is the prospect going to get from you and your opportunity? Make sure to include a phone number so that the most interested can contact you quickly. Take a look at a card I use, a card which has already generated thousands of responses.

This card does the following:

- establishes the market — all coffee drinkers. That's the qualifier.

- provides chief benefit in the headline "FREE GOURMET COFFEE FOR LIFE". There's no fooling around here with what the prospect gets.

- establishes secondary market — people wanting to cash in on the $11 billion coffee market.

- provides a list of secondary benefits (beyond free coffee and income) including free membership, direct shipments, *etc*.

- utilizes another one of the prospect's senses by providing information about flavors. Good marketing brings in as many of the five senses as possible.

This is a lot to pack onto a postcard… but the results prove this hard-hitting client-centered approach works.

If you're going to create this kind of card yourself, be smart:

- gather a bunch of card-decks and remove the opportunity cards;

- spread them out on the kitchen table, at least a dozen of them;

- review them carefully to see what catches your eye, what seems to work. Ask yourself what cards you'd respond to — and why;

- if you're particularly well-organized, get on the phone and call the advertiser. Ask him whether the card worked… and what he thinks would have improved it, (after all, he's had experience in the business you haven't had yet);

- then take two pieces of 8 1/2" x 11" paper. One represents the front of the card, the second's the back;

- block out the two sides so that all the things you need to have on the card are in fact there, namely

Side 1 (color side)

Your phone number for immediate service

Headline with your best benefit in it

Reasons why prospect should contact you... benefits you have for him

Any special offer you're making available for immediate action

Side 2

Divide this side into two parts. Divide the card horizontally, with between 50-60% going to the first section.

In section 1,

- put a box and ask the prospect to affirm that he/she wants your chief benefit;
- get any other information you need (like "Are you in an MLM now? If so, which one?" Or, "do you have MLM experience and an existing downline? If so, how many people in your organization?" This is part of the qualifying information you need.
- then ask for the prospect's name, address, phone (day and evening) and fax.

Make sure to request clear printing since people's handwriting is abysmal these days — and, of course, make it clear there can be no response without a phone number.

In section 2,

- put a box for the stamp
- include your phone number again with the words "for faster service call"
- provide your name and return address.

A Plea

Unless you're familiar with card-decks, don't get too creative. In every issue, there's some yokel who (despite never having run a card-deck in his life) decides he knows 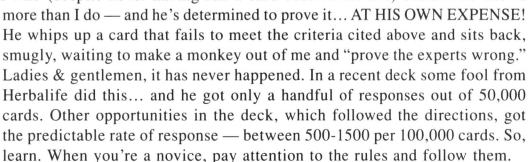 more than I do — and he's determined to prove it... AT HIS OWN EXPENSE! He whips up a card that fails to meet the criteria cited above and sits back, smugly, waiting to make a monkey out of me and "prove the experts wrong." Ladies & gentlemen, it has never happened. In a recent deck some fool from Herbalife did this... and he got only a handful of responses out of 50,000 cards. Other opportunities in the deck, which followed the directions, got the predictable rate of response — between 500-1500 per 100,000 cards. So, learn. When you're a novice, pay attention to the rules and follow them.

Note: writing a winning card isn't difficult, but experience definitely helps. In this connection, when people order space in my card-deck, I offer them two kinds of copy assistance. For those who want deluxe treatment, I refer them to the National Copywriting Center where our experienced copywriters will create the card from scratch for a very reasonable fee. I send the more budget-minded a series of successful business opportunity cards and urge them to draft the front and back of their cards. They then fax their draft to me, and I edit their work at no charge until we are both happy with the result.

Once we are, it's time to consider doing the art work. Creating camera-ready art is the step beyond copy. Camera-ready art is what the printer prints from, and it must be done in certain ways which include:

- screened film negatives, right reading, emulsion side down, 120-line screen

- veloxes/Linotronic RC paper/laser output

- within a specific image area, no bleeds.

Frankly, unless you're design proficient yourself, I suggest you hire my old friend and associate John Hamwey to do your camera-ready art. John's been designing all kinds of stuff for me for years, including my card-deck cards. Contact John at (617) 575-9915. Line busy? It's probably me.

2) Get prepared for the response. One of the things that never ceases to astonish me is when people order a card, are told what kind of response to expect — but fail to get ready to respond promptly. You'd think this kind of business masochism would be rare — but it isn't! Time after time, my advertisers sheepishly confess that they weren't ready for the predicted response and had to gear up — *after* the responses were already coming in. This is idiocy!!! You've got to prepare yourself *before* the deck drops so you can focus on responding as soon as your leads come in.

This means making sure you have a qualifying phone script. When calls come in, they are "suspects", people who *might* buy your opportunity. But, until you've got further information, you just don't know. That's why you've got to take this opportunity to ask some probing qualifying questions. Don't just ask for the prospect's name, address, and telephone number. Find out what you need to know to ensure that this is the kind of person you really want to risk any more time and money on. Here are some things to help:

▮ presume the prospect wants to give you his/her phone number. Say, "What are your phone and fax numbers?," *not* "Can I have your phone and fax numbers?"

■ if the person won't provide you with a telephone number, say, "I'm sorry, but our distributors need a phone number to be able to discuss the program with you. We won't be able to work with you without it." If the suspect still refuses to provide this information, end the conversation politely. He's not a real prospect.

■ if the person refuses to answer any questions say, "Our distributors need this information to do their work properly. If you can't supply it, we won't be able to work with you." Again, trust your gut. If you can't get the information you and your downline need, terminate the conversation politely, but firmly.

■ if you ask a question like, "If all your questions are satisfactorily answered about this opportunity, are you prepared to join right away?" and the prospect gives an unsatisfactory or evasive question, you're not dealing with a real prospect at all, and should proceed accordingly.

In short, when a person calls you for information, you've been provided a golden opportunity to question this individual about his situation and intentions. Take it. I recently heard of a case where an individual ran his opportunity in a card-deck and received about 750 responses. He didn't bother to do any qualifying of his responses. Instead, he assembled an expensive package that cost $3 between contents and mailing costs and blithely sent it off. He signed up just 13 people out of 750, and took a real bath. This foolish advertiser made a very elementary mistake, assuming that a *suspect* was a *prospect*... that is, that a person who had spent about 1 minute reviewing and sending in a business reply card was a real prospect, instead of someone who needed to be qualified before the proper response could be determined.

3) Sign up your first recruit as soon as possible. If you couldn't co-op the card and were forced to assume its total burden for yourself this one time only, then you've got to get some help right away. Thus, make prospects a special offer: if they sign up within 7 days of receipt of your materials, you'll provide them with 25 free leads! In other words, turn your lemons (all the leads you've got coming in) into lemonade (a means of building the organizations of your first distributors).

To make this situation work, you need to be well prepared.

• If you're smart, you've worked with us to put your entire case into a self-mailer flyer. Thus, as soon as you've signed up your first distributor (and, remember, while your leads are still coming in) you can have your self-mailer personalized with your new recruit's name, address, phone and company i.d. number. Thus, he'll have prospects to mail to and his mailing piece all ready to go. This is very smart marketing.

- If you haven't done a self-mailer (a mistake), you need to make sure your new recruit gets the materials he needs to be able to make a persuasive presentation to the leads you're providing him. These materials should include:

  - a sheet listing the five top reasons for joining your opportunity;

  - information on how the prospect will make money and otherwise benefit;

  - detailed instructions for building up an organization.

In other words, you need a sales kit.

Note: At the same time you sign up your first recruit into your program, sign him/her up for a share of card-deck leads (in other words you can provide 25 free... and sell a share of those remaining. $2.00 a lead is a reasonable price under the circumstances.) Too, sign your recruit into Ad-Net to ensure that he has additional leads coming in shortly. Since the Ad-Net leads take about 30 days to begin, it is especially sensible to get card-deck leads into your recruit's hands ASAP. Finally, make sure your recruit understands that it is his responsibility not only to sign up his prospects into your main opportunity but, simultaneously, to sell card-deck shares and an Ad-Net, Inc. membership. If you do not provide your recruits with an ongoing supply of leads you are ensuring both their failure — and yours!

4) Replicate The Process. When I first came into network marketing, I made a classic error. Since I had no problem recruiting people, I just kept adding them to my first line until it was well over 100 strong. Because I was inexperienced I thought that others would be as masterful recruiters as I was... and that they'd get on with their recruiting game as well as I was getting on with mine. Wrong! For lots of reasons (including lack of experience, lack of leads, lack of recruiting prowess and just plain sloth and laziness), most of these people, once recruited, settled back to do — NOTHING! I was flabbergasted. But I learned...

... I learned the correct way of building an organization. Now, I bring in a person on my first line and insist that he:

- join Ad-Net immediately. A person who won't join Ad-Net, and so ensure his supply of leads, is unwelcome in my organization.

- take a share of one of our many co-ops. He needs to i) send in his monthly Ad-Net certificate to our space-ad co-op program; ii) purchase a share in one of my Staff of Life and Gourmet Coffee Club card-deck co-ops, and/or iii) purchase a share in one of our card-deck Ad-Net co-ops that generate leads for the development of Ad-Net organizations. (Remember, Ad-Net is a network marketing opportunity, too, and as such you need leads for it.)

▮ set a precise objective about how many people he'll recruit each month, each quarter. One per month (as per "The Awesome Power of One") is the minimum acceptable... and for people who think of themselves as "heavy hitters" it should be many more! (By the way, it's a good idea to be very skeptical about the so-called "heavy hitters" and their recruiting prowess. I've got one in my Staff of Life organization who promised big things, but nearly a year after being recruited his grand total stands at one person sponsored. The fact is, he's a wind bag, as so many of these people are.)

▮ recruit a person and then assist this person get started, which means assisting this person into Ad-Net, the various co-op programs, *etc.*; in short that you assist this individual replicate success.

Since I have instituted this unrelenting and completely professional approach, several very important developments have occurred:

1) the MLM time wasters, many of whom flocked to join my organization in the beginning, have largely dropped out. These people are the notorious "fleas", the people who jump from opportunity to opportunity, aimlessly searching for the one that's going to make them rich without any work. They had all been in many, even dozens, of other opportunities before joining with me... and no doubt, they will be in many, even dozens, of others before the grim reaper puts them out of their peripatetic misery. I am glad to be rid of them, not least because these people constantly whined for services... but did nothing to help themselves achieve success. They are a menace to the industry and, like biblical locusts, a plague on the land.

2) my organization has been re-populated by professional, business people. I like these people... I understand them. I am, after all, one myself. One of the great things that I like about them is that they don't expect something for nothing, they are used to working hard and they are very interested in a *systematic* approach to success. They know that success takes time, money and effort. They are not unwilling to invest these... so long as they can be reasonably assured that success will follow. What's more, unlike the MLM locusts, they are not passive. They are active participants in their fate. As such, they are not only willing to work the system... they take the time to make suggestions for improving it. While there are many fewer such people in this category than amongst the fleas... they are better to work with. Thus, the first line of my organization is actually smaller now than when I was furiously recruiting people in my early days... but the organization overall is immensely stronger.

3) This is true for one other reason: I now bring in one and make sure he can replicate the process as noted above... before recruiting another. I am no

longer merely interested in bodies... I want people who will work with me to replicate a successful process. And during the inevitable qualifying conversations that take place between me and any individual prospect before he signs up, I make it absolutely clear what I expect from people in my organization. People new to opportunities, or people without either sufficient self-esteem or an understanding of the process of how to make money in network marketing, are unwilling to question prospects and make their standards plain, feeling sure that such probing will result in the prospect first taking umbrage and then taking flight.

This, of course, is ridiculous. While it is certainly true that a new recruit must understand as much as possible about his leader (and if you substitute the word "leader" for "upline", you realize how ill-equipped most of these upline people are to be supplying assistance to anyone) and about the leader's system... it is equally true that the leader must know what he can expect from his recruit. Thus, the leader has a right and duty to ask candid, focused, probing questions and to demand equally candid, focused, detailed responses. Unless there is this kind of clarity at the beginning, the relationship (like most of those in the opportunity industry) is doomed from the start.

Note: There's no disgrace in starting small in card-decks, with just 50,000 cards. There's no disgrace in having to pay for your first card yourself. That's a perfectly legitimate business investment. However, there's a big problem with *staying* small... and continuing to plow money into an opportunity that isn't working. As a result of your first card-deck insertion, you should be recruiting at least enough people to pay for a full run of 100,000 cards in a second issue. This means recruiting at least 14 people each of whom pays $100. If you can't do this, there's either a problem with your "opportunity" or there's a problem with your recruiting system. Review both and take the necessary steps to improve matters. Once you're determined your system is successful, expand it. Don't wait. Your objective, mind, is to run in *every* appropriate card-deck as well as all other appropriate lead-generating vehicles. Do so. To this end, I'd be happy to assist you. One of my hats is that of card-deck broker. I can place your opportunity card in any deck for a price hundreds, even thousands of dollars lower than you can get yourself. For more information on getting the maximum number of cards for free and building your organization rapidly, see my Special Report #R139, HOW I GET 10,000,000+ FREE POST CARDS EVERY YEAR TO BOOST MY MLM ORGANIZATIONS... HOW YOU CAN, TOO!, page 138.

Another Way To Benefit From Card-Decks: Getting The People In Your Ad-Net Organization To Create Card-Deck Co-ops

Just in case it isn't entirely clear to you by now, what you're trying to do in MLM is *leverage* the responses of people in your organization to increase both their wealth

— and yours. Towards this end, here's a card-deck-based means of developing wealth that the other industry "gurus" have entirely overlooked.

As I've stressed throughout, one of the ways to make real money through your network marketing opportunity is to join Ad-Net. If you don't, you're making a very serious mistake. Here's why...

- If you're not in Ad-Net and you ask someone to be in your opportunity, they're either going to say yes or no. Chances are, they're going to refuse, since far more people will decline to join rather than become a team-member. That's life.

- When you join Ad-Net, however, your options expand dramatically. Now if they say that they'll join your opportunity, you can sign them up into Ad-Net right away. They should do it; after all, they need a regular source of leads. Thus, you'll derive two checks each month from this person — instead of just one. This is the beginning of leverage. This person will now go on to sponsor others into both your opportunity and into Ad-Net *simultaneously.*

- both you and the people you sign up will, however, encounter far more people who won't join your primary network marketing opportunity than those who will. If, however, they are in ANOTHER MLM opportunity, you can still recruit them into Ad-Net since 100% of the people you encounter in another opportunity need a constant lead source not only for themselves but for members of their organization.

- Once the person is in Ad-Net, it's in your best interest to assist this person to promote *his* primary MLM vigorously. How's that? Well, mate, it stands to reason that if everyone this person signs up into his primary MLM can also be signed up into *your* Ad-Net organization, you want him to be a smash success in recruiting for his primary opportunity. One way of ensuring this success is to get this person into card decks via co-ops.

- Tell each person in your Ad-Net organization that you're familiar with a card-deck that will generate between 500-1500 leads for him every 90 days. Urge him to create a co-op and sell shares in the responses. Since my deck costs just $1399 for 100,000 two-color cards, each of the 14 shares should cost $100. Or, sell shares for as little as $70 and sell twice as many. Divide all incoming leads into shares for all the advertisers and one additional one for yourself or the organizer as payment for services.

- Make sure that as all shareholders send out the marketing communications on their primary MLM, they include details on Ad-Net; (our Ad-Net self-mailer is perfect for this).

- When the people in the co-op sign up new recruits, they should immediately sign them up into Ad-Net — and for a share of the next co-op, thus assisting in the growth and continuation of the organizational model.

Thus, the money of the 14 paid shareholders not only provides leveraged income for the co-op organizer... but for you, too.

Note: It behooves you to think long and seriously about the leveraging concept. You'll find it a recurring theme of this book. In the case of co-ops, consider how powerful this is. Thanks to the leads coming in from just one deck, the organizer's organization will grow. He should, therefore, be able not only to purchase another card in Card Deck I — but expand into other card-decks. Which is, of course, the objective. Your job is not only to place your own primary MLM in all card decks... but to assist the people in your Ad-Net organization (who are working another primary MLM) to be in those decks, too. In this way you'll experience dynamic growth for the least out-of-pocket expense!!!

Resource

As proprietor of the nation's biggest and least-expensive card-deck, I'm in a position to assist you and members of your organization reap the benefits of card-decks.

- If you're in any other organization other than Gourmet Coffee Club and The Staff of Life (which are already fully integrated into my and other card-decks), contact me right away to place your card.

- Then identify the MLM programs of *all* the people in your Ad-Net organization. If they're in your primary MLM, sell them a co-op share. If they're not, encourage them to organize their own card-deck co-op for their primary MLM. Make sure they know about our Ad-Net self-mailers (as mentioned above, Robert Blackman will be happy to send a self-mailer sampler pack for just $3 if you haven't seen one) and how to integrate them into the marketing packages for their primary MLM. In other words, show them the benefits of taking a leveraged approach to this business.

For further information on how to use card-decks to your advantage, contact me at (617) 547-6372. And, remember, don't go into anyone's deck without consulting me. As a card-deck publisher and broker, I can ordinarily get you prices that are far lower than the other decks will quote you if you approach them directly.

∎ Lead-Generator (Bingo) Cards

This same concept, of course, applies to lead-generator (or "bingo") cards. Here's what they look like:

As you can see by perusing this example, the offers of lots of network marketing opportunities appear on cards like these. No wonder. While bingo cards don't produce leads that are as strong as those coming from full card-deck cards, bingo cards are still very useful in organizational growth and development — if you use them properly.

Lots of people have dropped off bingo cards because they don't understand how they work. Here are some helpful hints so you get the best results:

- Co-op your leads from these cards at reasonable cost. As you see, my prices are about the lowest in the industry; at least I haven't seen anything lower! I charge a flat rate of $90. Given that the lowest number of leads anyone's going to get is about 40 (350 is our record so far), this means that in a worst-case scenario your leads are going to cost a little more than $2 each. A large percentage of them come with phone numbers; we certainly always ask for them!

- Arrange with several members of your organization to purchase leads from you for, say, $1.50 each. This allows you to cover your costs on the deal.

- Then go ahead and book your space on the lead-generating card. Remember, it can take up to 6 weeks before you start getting leads. So, plan ahead.

- We send all leads to a single source — you or whomever you designate. We print them via laser printer. If you've involved others in your co-op, this format makes it easy to divide the prospect leads and distribute them. Before using them, make sure either to 1) add the names to your mailing list or 2) make a copy so you can get back to them. Don't just mail and throw the list away! Remember, these names (like all leads) are subject to the Rule of 7. If you mail without inputting the data in your computer, you're making a very serious mistake. After all, prospects must be hit a minimum of 7 times!!! (This is a basic rule of marketing. If the entire subject of marketing is new to you, check out my book MONEY MAKING MARKETING: FINDING THE PEOPLE WHO NEED WHAT YOU'RE SELLING AND MAKING SURE THEY BUY IT.)

- Once you've got the leads, divide them into the most sensible divisions. In other words, send people in Ohio leads from Ohio (or at least the Mid-West); send women the leads from women, *etc*. In short, use your discretion about who gets what leads. **Note**: if the lead has no phone number, it's not a good lead at all. Unless you've got a lot of extra money you don't know what else to do with, don't bother dealing with this lead at all.

- In sending these leads, remind people in your organization how to work them. Just like all leads, these need to be pre-qualified. Novices in the lead-generation field customarily err by getting a lead (with or without phone number) and simply mailing their marketing package out without further ado. This is a mistake. Before investing any more time and money in a "prospect", make sure he's real. Get on the phone and pre-qualify. If you can't get on the phone, send the prospect a brief letter or post card setting forth the advantages of your program and asking the prospect either to send you a phone number so you can be in touch... or to call you to get started. In short, don't treat a person like a prospect... until he's clearly demonstrated to you that he is in fact a prospect.

Note: As you know, I've found in practice that it's a very good idea to send a memo along with these names in which you clearly set forth what you want the people in your organization to do when they receive the names. This memo should include the following items:

- Here is your latest shipment of prospect leads for /name of your program/.

- These leads need to be pre-qualified. Call them ASAP to ensure that they are in fact interested in getting involved in a business opportunity, have the resources to do so and will work with us to build a lucrative organization. If not, don't bother to send anything!!!

- If you've received a lead without a phone number, it's not a good lead. Send a post card or memo indicating the benefits of our program and ask that this person either send you a phone number so you can get in touch... or ask him to call you. A person who's been asked to provide a phone number but who has failed to do so isn't a good prospect and should be treated accordingly.

- Once you've pre-qualified your leads, send out the marketing materials ASAP. Then follow up when you said you were going to. (You did arrange a time for following up, didn't you?)

- If the person is interested in signing up into our opportunity, make sure he/she signs up into Ad-Net, too.

- If the person signs up in our opportunity, make sure to sign him/her up in our next lead-generating co-op program, including the one from the lead-generating card.

- If the person won't sign up into our primary network marketing opportunity, but is working *another* opportunity, make sure he signs up into Ad-Net. Then explain how this person should be growing his organization by using Jeffrey Lant's and other card-decks. (**Note**: I will be happy to send information on our card-deck and other lead-generating programs to all people in your organization if you either send me their names and addresses and the names of their programs... or give them my phone number and ask them to get in touch.)

- Ask your new recruit to send you at least a copy of his completed application for the primary MLM program and a copy of his Ad-Net application. This way you'll know that he has followed through. If you don't receive these materials by an agreed-upon date (say, 5 business days from this call), follow up again to expedite matters.

Note: One thing I've learned in MLM is not to be afraid to keep hammering the same points home month after month. It's not enough just to send people in your organization leads. You've got to send them the guidelines for following up these leads... and then you've got to send them again. Thus, have these guidelines available on computer or photo copy a couple dozen sheets so that each time you send out prospect leads, you can send the guidelines for working them, too!

Resource

All card decks run bingo cards and many other print publications do, too. The best way to find sources to run your ad, therefore, is simply to go through decks and pull out the bingo cards. You can, of course, start with my deck... and my bingo card. You're certain to want to use this resource! To be certain you're reviewed all decks, again check the listing in *Standard Rate & Data*. Develop a form letter on computer in which you ask for information on the bingo card, the set-up charge, the cost per lead, how leads are made available, and any other pertinent information. If you call to ask me for these details, I have a detailed letter fully explaining how bingo cards work and the best way to use them.

Companies Which Generate Leads

In addition to space ads and card-deck ads, if you're going to be a success in network and opportunity marketing, you've got to be familiar with the various companies that generate leads and provide them to you on a regular basis. The reason is plain: as your organization grows, it's going to need more and still more leads. You must, therefore, familiarize yourself with *all* lead-generating mechanisms. The two key words here are "familiarize" and "all."

In just the last few years several entrepreneurs came to the understanding that all network and opportunity marketers needed leads and that there was probably as much money, if not more, to be made in providing these marketers with this essential... than there was in developing any single opportunity. It's the same mentality that lead people during the California gold rush to set up grocery stores, hard-ware stores, and saloons for the miners... instead of venturing out into the wilderness in pursuit of the big hit. For these people the money's not in finding the gold but providing the pick ax to get it out of the ground.

Unfortunately, the theory is better than the practice. Here's what I mean by this:

- a person who's selling names to MLM and opportunity marketers ought to be selling the names of people who have explicitly and recently requested business opportunity details;
- the information provided ought to be keyed in properly, so that it's usable;
- entries ought to include phone numbers, and
- data must be sent promptly to the marketer.

On this basis, most companies fail.

No wonder. As you'll see from the detailed analyses below, most network marketing companies whose product line is selling leads to people in other network marketing opportunities have severe flaws in their businesses, to wit:

- nearly all rely on mailing lists for their names, rather than getting their prospect leads in response to ads. In this case, companies rent lists from people like me who do a lot of opportunity advertising; (I've been approached, you see, to rent my list. I've refused). The catch is the people on these lists may or (more usually) may not be in the market just now for an opportunity. Worse, the list owner may keep names on his list too long, may not clean the list, and/or may be sloppy about data entry. The net result is that the list can well be old and of very uneven quality. **Note**: several of my Tele-Close clients have gotten leads from Co-Op Lead Network, a network marketing company that sells leads. On one list of 300 names, 1/3 had bad phone numbers. In one case, the party in question hadn't lived at the number provided for about 4 years. This proves my point precisely. Where you're renting names from mailing lists instead of those of recent responders to opportunity ads, you're buying a pig in a poke. You know what that means!

- none of these companies has input the vast majority of their data. Nor can they tell you when the data was input, how recent it is, or how valuable. In short, the companies are taking as much a risk as you are... except the companies know they can minimize their risk by selling this poor-quality data to you!

- companies don't have the resources or have otherwise made the decision not to engage in a strenuous advertising program to generate prospect leads. Face it. If you want fresh prospect leads, you've got to advertise for them. Yet the truth is very few companies go out and secure the bulk of their names from continuous advertising programs. The best of these is Ad-Net.

During the writing of this resource, one of my friends advised me to avoid making specific recommendations of companies, resources, *etc.* in this book in case the situation in regard to that company changes. He certainly doesn't know me very well!!!

As anyone knows who is familiar with my many books, my resources are studded with specific references... it's my privilege, you see, to be in a position to be able to review dozens, even hundreds of specific items. And I feel utterly no compunction or hesitation about telling you what I think about any and all of them. As you may imagine, the companies whose products I find lacking don't particularly care for what I've written. But that's their problem. They should have been more careful before recommending a substandard product to the world. By the same token, I have absolutely no problem saying that a particular company is good — if it is. And if I'm benefiting from saying so, that's no problem either... so long as I'm up front about it. So, let me tell you right now: after a thorough review of the companies selling leads and set up in a direct marketing fashion, I came to the conclusion that Ad-Net is a company I feel happy recommending.

Let me explain how I reached this conclusion, and why I think you'll want to participate as actively in Ad-Net as I do; so actively that I am now the #1 distributor in the entire company!

Six Lead-Generating MLM Companies

My research has uncovered six lead-generating network marketing companies. Of these we can review (and discard) the first four right away:

1) Co-op Lead Network, 1821 Hall Ave., Suite 20, Marinette, WI 54143 (715) 735-6869

2) Focus 1000, Cottonwood Professional Plaza, 1927 East 5600 South, P.O. Box 21276, Salt Lake City, UT 84121 (801) 277-0744. (Says they use "pre-tested mailing lists" but didn't tell me anything more than that.)

3) Prospects Unlimited, 9501 Rodney Parham Road, Suite 208, Little Rock, AR 72207 (501) 223-4999

4) United Prosper Club, 11926 W. Temple Dr., Morrison, CO 80465 (303) 932-0089; (800) 442-0349.

   (Note: in all fairness I should say that CEO Fred Condra tells me all leads generated by this company are called by telemarketers to confirm prospect interest.)

5) Pro-Step, P.O. Box 5678, Destin, FL 32540-5678 800-656-7767

6) Ad-Net. See page 130.

— Why The First Four Have To Go

As you already know, I am keen that all people in your organization have the best possible prospect leads. They are an essential element of success. Now, all four companies would probably tell you at the drop of the hat that they have the best leads. But they're all primarily based on one principle: renting you mailing lists. That is, when you subscribe to their services what you're really doing is renting lists from them that they have rented from others. This is, I think, a dubious proposition.

Why? Because when you rent a mailing list you're never quite sure of what you're getting. List owners, as I know from my work in the card-deck and catalog business, can often be careless about their lists. They leave names on too long and don't delete old or doubtful data. Indeed, either out of laziness or to fatten their rental checks, they leave these names on and rent them for years after any value they've had is gone.

What's more, the people on these lists may or may not have responded to an offer like yours. Or they may have found an opportunity they're happy with, or been so burned by their selection that they've dropped out of the opportunity market altogether.

Unfortunately, you can quiz neither the list owner nor renter about what you're getting as you can when you rent lists directly. If I'm renting a list for my catalog or card deck, for instance, I can keep pressing the owner or broker until I get the details I need before investing my money. If I don't hear what I need to hear, I don't have to go ahead. But that's not true with the first four companies. You've got to take whatever they dish out.

In fairness, the MLM may not like this, either, but you're the guy paying for the inadequate prospect names.

Under these circumstances, these companies are just too risky for me. And, in fact, I've seen real problems with several of them. In one case, for instance, I saw a mailing list provided to a member where every name started with the letter "S"; this clearly was not a response list, but a mailing list. In another, about 40% of the phone numbers were wrong and in one case the party told us that the man in question was dead and hadn't lived at that address for years. This is a typical mailing list problem, and that's why you should be very, very careful before you get involved with any company based on lists.

Two Better Choices

That leaves us with two other choices, Pro-Step and Ad-Net.

These companies do have certain similarities, and no wonder. The founder and CEO of Pro-Step, Kevin Lehmann, used to be a senior executive at Ad-Net. As such he knew the Ad-Net method backwards and forwards. Thus, when he got the itch to have his own company he was able, at first, to set up a company that offered some competitive advantages to Ad-Net and as such he made a bit of a stir in the industry.

HOW TO SUCCEED IN AD-NET

- Select the number of prospect leads you can *call* each month — 30, 50 or 100. The days are long gone (if, indeed, they ever existed) when you can simply mail your way to success. You've got to talk to people.

- When you get your leads, call them immediately. Note: all Ad-Net leads have telephone numbers.

- When you get the prospects on the phone, qualify them. If you're selling a commodity (like we are in Gourmet Coffee Club, for instance), ask if they already use it. If so, ask them to try yours. Once they start using (and liking) a commodity, it's much easier to upgrade them to sell it. Alternatively, ask them if they're looking for an opportunity. If not, don't press but ring off politely. If they say they are, then make sure they've got what it takes to make it work: time, money, determination. If you like what you hear, say you'll send your sales information. Don't end the conversation without scheduling a follow-up call. Note: If your prospects say they're not interested in your primary opportunity, show them the benefits of Ad-Net. Remind them every person in their organization needs leads and that helping their downline get these leads is a crucial way to ensuring their own success. Also, point out the benefits to them of recruiting their company into Ad-Net!

- When you send the information out (that day preferably) put in a note confirming the time you'll follow up and stressing any key benefits of your opportunity.

- Follow up when you were going to. If the person isn't available and has an answering machine say, "Sorry I missed our scheduled appointment. I called to give you <prime benefit of the opportunity you're promoting.> Either call me back at <your number> to reschedule, or I'll try you at this same time tomorrow."

- When you get your prospect on the phone, ask immediately if he/she is ready to sign up. Don't oversell. If people are ready now (and some will be), move to complete the paperwork, giving them preliminary information on how to recruit, *etc.* Make sure they sign up not only into your primary opportunity, but into Ad-Net, too. Remember, your recruits need prospects!

- If your prospect isn't ready to sign up, ask why. Answer his/her questions and provide necessary information. If you're ever in doubt about the seriousness of this person, say "What will it take for you to sign up TODAY?" If what you hear is reasonable, do it. If not, say so. Don't waste time with the unserious!

- Set your objective for the month. Your minimum objective (under the "Awesome Power of One" System) is to recruit at least one new person and to make sure that each person in your organization recruits one additional person, too. Remember, getting one new person out of the 30, 50, or 100 leads Ad-Net provides monthly isn't difficult; the more months you work at it, the easier it will get and the higher your success rate! Remember, one is a minimum goal!

- Use your Ad-Net certificates to get more prospect leads. Ask your company for camera-ready art. If they don't have any (all too common), either develop it yourself, or call me at The National Copywriting Center (617) 547-6372 for assistance.

- One last thing. If, upon signing up, your new Ad-Net member sends me $3, he/she'll get detailed instructions on how to be successful and recruit the maximum number of people. Your prospects will also get my quarterly catalog which contains many useful assistance tools. Make sure both you and your recruits stay in touch with me. I'm happy to help you all build the largest possible organizations!

Like Ad-Net, for instance, he offered names that were fresh and came in response to network marketing ads. Indeed, his ads specifically generated people interested in network marketing. (Note: I have to say that this didn't hold much water with me. I don't believe that a person has to be interested in network marketing to succeed in MLM. The person only has to be interested in a business opportunity and in following directions in a businesslike way. I've never been interested in limiting my market to just MLM types. I want intelligent, organized, go-ahead entrepreneurial types, whether they know anything about MLM or not; thus, I found the Pro-Step prospect lead focus too narrow for my taste.)

Lehmann also publishes a good training newsletter and provides interactive training calls. Initially, Lehmann also offered more monthly leads than Ad-Net (100), although his cost was also higher ($100 per month). On this basis, Lehmann enjoyed a nice little surge, and I got a lot of calls to join Pro-Step.

But, in all seriousness, there wasn't any reason to do so, especially when CEO Jim Wingo added a series of improvements to Ad-Net that again made it head and shoulders the best lead-generating company in the industry.

Here are the reasons why Ad-Net is superior:

- where the leads come from. The prospect names you get from Ad-Net are fresh and looking for a business opportunity. These leads come from many places, including card decks, space ads, *etc*. Note: even though these leads are good, that doesn't mean you can simply send your sales materials to them without qualifying them. In my view, it's always a good idea to phone people and ensure that they're looking for a business opportunity and will look seriously at yours before you send anything. That's why a phone number is crucial. All Ad-Net leads have phone numbers so you can pre-qualify and follow up accordingly.

- different sized packages of prospect leads. In Pro-Step you must take 100 leads monthly; that's all they offer. In Ad-Net, you can select 30, 50 or 100 leads. I think this makes more sense. Frankly, unless you're a full-time entrepreneur, it may well be difficult to follow up 100 leads each month — unless you forego the crucial pre-qualifying mentioned above. That's a mistake. You may find that you only have time to work with 30 or 50 leads. Of course, people like me get the 100 leads monthly, but you can still succeed (if not to the maximum extent) by working fewer leads and following "The Awesome Power of One" system.

- how leads are sent. Ad-Net makes leads available on handy pressure-sensitive labels, which are most easy to use. Pro-Step doesn't.

- free ad certificates. One big plus for Ad-Net has always been the fact that it issues all active members free ad certificates. You can use these to generate still more prospect leads. Importantly, unlike the main leads (which in both Pro-Step and Ad-Net are shared with a certain number of other members) the leads you generate from these ads are yours alone. Just provide the publishers of selected publications with the ad certificate and camera ready art (which, by the way, we can provide for you through The National Copywriting Center), and you'll get more leads. Moreover, you can pool the certificates from people in your group to get bigger ads with more impact.

- discount advertising. Ad-Net's objective is to get you the maximum number of leads possible. That's why, in addition to the free advertising certificates, they also offer a discount advertising program that Pro-Step doesn't have.

Additional Ad-Net benefits (so far unmatched by Pro-Step) include both free voice mail and personalized fax on demand. And like Pro-Step it also offers a solid training newsletter, where you'll generally find an article by me.

For these reasons, while I certainly admire Kevin Lehmann and have always found him a hard-working entrepreneur, I am happy to stick with Ad-Net and recommend it to you. Ad-Net is the original prospect lead generating MLM and, with six years experience in business, remains the largest and most solid.

Yes, Ad-Net is the best bet by far among the lead-generating network marketing companies and as such you should join it, specifically in my organization. Do I have a vested interest in saying so? Of course. I am now the company's only Diamond Executive, the #1 distributor. And I must say I intend to retain this position and keep my income for life.

You're going to help me do so. Not, I hope, merely by recruiting one person at a time, the old fashioned way. Let me be candid with you. I haven't gotten to be the #1 distributor in Ad-Net by recruiting one person at a time. I've gotten there by using leverage, bringing in entire companies which then promote Ad-Net to ALL their members. As these members sign up, and follow my recommended recruiting techniques (on which I advise the companies), my organization grows by hundreds. Which is just the way it ought to be.

Ad-Net, to my knowledge (and I must say, thanks to me), is recommended by more MLM companies to their distributors than any other lead-generating company. Period. This process is calling leveraging, and it's something you can benefit from, too, to break free of laborious one on one recruiting... and start recruiting hundreds at a time.

How Leveraging Will Put Hundreds Of People Into Your Ad-Net Organization Fast And Build It Regularly

But there's more — and here's where leverage starts to make its awesome impact truly felt.

Once you've recruited someone into Ad-Net (who's working another opportunity and won't join your primary opportunity), you can start working with this person, this person's organization and its economic power to achieve truly startling results.

- Start by sponsoring your recruit's entire downline into Ad-Net. The best way to do this is to have your recruit sponsor his entire first line... then have people on his first line sponsor all the people on their first line, *etc.* until your original recruit's entire organization has been sponsored. This is step one.

- Then escalate. Have your new recruit recruit *his* immediate upline sponsor. Once this has happened, make sure this upline sponsor recruits (line by line as above) *his* entire organization into Ad-Net;

- Then your immediate upline sponsor should recruit *his* immediate upline sponsor, and so on until this entire leg of the organization has been captured.

Getting the picture? There's even more...

- Say you're in network marketing opportunity A and recruit someone into Ad-Net who's in network marketing opportunity B. Every person that this person recruits into Ad-Net is someone to your benefit. Thus, you want him/her to engage in the most strenuous outreach and recruitment possible. One way of doing this, as already suggested, is through card-decks. Urge your new recruit in opportunity B to put together a card-deck co-op lead-generating program. Tell him he can get FREE leads if he'll organize the co-op (always cutting himself in for a free share), collect the money, place the card, *etc.* If the card is placed in a deck like mine mailed to 100,000 prospects, information about *your* Ad-Net organization will be sent to all the respondents (numbering, remember, between 1/2-1.5% of the total mailed). Your organization thus grows — at no cost to you and at the cost of only "sweat equity" to the card-deck co-op organizer.

- This fabulous system, as I've said, can and should be extended into both other card-decks and into space-ads as well for further desirable results.

One More Way To Leverage

If you're smart you've now seen the dramatic reasons why you need to work Ad-Net along with your regular program and you understand why you can build a very sizable

Ad-Net organization much quicker than you can with your primary opportunity. But there's another way to achieve breathtaking growth that you should be aware of: signing up chief executive officers and the company itself into Ad-Net.

The system I've previously mentioned will enable you to take over companies from the very bottom. In other words, what I said above will enable you to recruit organizations and companies into Ad-Net starting from ground zero. Here you can use the very newest, greenest recruit to get started, so long as this person has the required upline sponsor. There's nothing wrong with this process. It produces very substantial results in short order... if you follow the directions. However, there is another, even more substantial way: recruit the company.

As I go to press, I now already recruited several network marketing CEOs into my Ad-Net program; their companies have over 35,000 independent distributors enrolled who are all being systematically recruited for my Ad-Net organization BY THE COMPANIES THEMSELVES. Technically, the CEOs have either signed up under their own Social Security number (for personal gain) or under their company's federal i.d. number (for the gain of the company). In either case, once they've signed up, they proceed (working down line by line) to recruit their entire company into Ad-Net... thus ensuring that their independent distributors have a continuing source of leads... and providing both themselves and these distributors with an additional profit center.

While I have personally recruited some of these CEOs, some of those now in my Ad-Net organization have been recruited as a result of the assistance of people like you... that is, people who understood the power of leveraging and want to profit from it like I do. Such people go to the CEOs of their companies and say, in essence, "Jeffrey Lant has a complete system that will benefit all the independent distributors in this company as well as you yourself. I'd like you to review his materials and see how he can assist us." I then send the very extensive materials of my L.A.N.T. SYSTEM™, including complete details on self-mailers, Tele-Close, and, of course, lead-generating, along with Ad-Net.

Most CEOs are ecstatic to learn about this system, and why not?

- They or their company benefit because they get a cut of the profits from the self-mailers. Thus, they get a new profit center while still being able to supply marketing communications inexpensively to all their members.

- They get a monthly check from Ad-Net as a commission for all members of their company participating.

- They get to control their corporate message. The company approves all the materials we create including self-mailers, computer diskettes, card-deck cards, bingo-card ads, space ads, distributor recruitment kits, *etc*. Nothing is ever sent out for distributor use without company approval.

- They ensure that all distributors get a regular source of leads.
- They raise their national visibility exponentially... what with the millions of self-mailers their distributors will be sending, the space ads, card-deck ads, bingo-card ads, *etc.*
- They help all independent distributors retain members of their downline... and sponsor new recruits.
- It gives the company a unique competitive advantage against other companies. Would you rather go with a company that has a complete independent distributor support package? Or one that approaches marketing and the independent distributor with the kind of negligence so utterly characteristic of this often lackluster industry? It's obvious, isn't it?

In short, it's a win (for the CEO and company) win (for the independent distributors) situation!

Under these circumstances, it's only the most witless of CEOs who fails to be interested in this unique system for himself/his company and his independent distributors and who won't see me and learn even more about how The L.A.N.T. SYSTEM™ will help. (Sadly, there are any number of witless CEOs in this industry). Good CEOs, after all, are always interested in doing what they can to support and sustain their independent distributor field force.

The good CEOs understand that their independent distributors need...

- compelling client-centered marketing communications that are inexpensive to purchase and use;
- a steady supply of leads, and
- telemarketing support to both qualify and close prospects.

Such people are quick to grasp the favorable implications of the process both for their independent distributors (who are made more effective in recruitment and thus more likely to stay in the company and produce towards its welfare) and themselves. (After all, look at how many ways the company makes money from The L.A.N.T. SYSTEM™.)

In short order, intelligent CEOs grasp the essence of the issue... they understand that at minimal initial investment to themselves (all soon recoverable), they can support both their independent distributors and create new profit centers for their company. Signing up into Ad-Net, for all that it's another network marketing company, is a very small step to take!

Dumb CEOs think differently. They continue to believe in some kind of twisted Darwinism... believing that their job is to recruit distributors, throw them into the wilds without support, and see who survives. Or as one CEO told me while I was writing this book, "I provide my distributors with a brochure on the company and let them figure out everything else for themselves." It's deeply ironic, of course, that this same man considers himself a liberal, a humanist, a man who loves and supports other people. Why, he's told me as much over and over again. In truth, he's a myopic, self-serving, marketing-retarded, unimaginative flatworm. But oh-so-characteristic of his ilk.

Dear reader, throughout these pages I have warned and re-warned you about properly assessing any opportunity with which you're thinking of becoming affiliated. Be hard-nosed, be hard-headed, scrutinize thoroughly, weigh carefully. The company you want to affiliate yourself with must be a company that fully supports you as an independent distributor... which does everything conceivable to think through your situation in the field and to develop and provide vehicles for assuring your success.

And one of these vehicles is Ad-Net!

Let Me Help You Leverage

If you want to profit by sponsoring an entire company into Ad-Net, I'm happy to work with you. First, show the CEO of your company this book (and specifically this section) and the L.A.N.T. SYSTEM™ brochure on pages 145-146. If he/she has half a brain, he'll recognize just how our system — including Ad-Net — can be of assistance to his company. If you want to benefit from the leveraging possibilities, you must pre-sell the CEO on the entire system. Then let me know what you've done and that the CEO is ready to listen to a complete presentation on how to profit from all aspects of The L.A.N.T. SYSTEM™. I'll be happy to send our complete package of support materials and then follow up with a call. Once the company is willing to sign up, you'll be signed up directly under the company as tangible thanks for your intelligent referral and pre-selling. *All* additional sign-ups from the company into Ad-Net can then follow directly under YOU — to your very considerable advantage. (Keep in mind that we work directly with the company to ensure that the company sends out Ad-Net applications and other informative material to each distributor. Our approach to recruiting independent distributors in the companies we have under contract is very thorough and precise... which means that more and more people are sponsored under you!)

And just how beneficial is this to you? Well, say you're in a moderate-sized company with just 10,000 distributors. And say that only 10% of them, or 1000, sign up into Ad-Net and start using the marketing system made available by the company, a very conservative projection. These 1000 people sponsored into YOUR Ad-Net organization would be worth at least $1000 PER WEEK to you. Additionally, this $1000 would grow... since all new recruits into the company would automatically be presented with Ad-Net information and most would sign up; additionally, those already in Ad-Net would also be out recruiting. Thus your monthly checks would grow nicely.

Could you stand such a substantial sum for the very minimal work of persuading the CEO of your company that he/she should do what is in the best interests of the company and each individual independent distributor? If so, get started. And be sure to keep me abreast of developments so that I can assist you in every way possible!

Note: Two things to keep in mind:

> 1) Please be aware that at any given time lots of eager-beaver distributors, readers of this book and those familiar with my system, may be approaching the CEO of any given network marketing company. The person we will select to sign up under the company is the one who does the most to facilitate the sign-up and who keeps in touch with me, reporting progress.

> 2) Don't just send me the name, address and phone number of any given networking marketing CEO and tell me to do your work for you. If you expect to be compensated by having all the Ad-Net sign-ups within a given company placed under you, you've got to do ALL the pre-qualifying and pre-selling. This is what you're being compensated for... and if you can't/won't do it, you can't expect generous compensation.

Very Important Note: There is no limit to the number of companies you can recruit and benefit from through this incredibly brilliant leveraging system. Consider *all* the people you know in *all* network marketing companies. Ask them if they know the CEO of their company... or would be willing to send a letter on behalf of The L.A.N.T. SYSTEM™ to their CEO. If so, make a deal with them. Agree that if the company adopts the entire system, you both will share a membership in Ad-Net; that the company will be sponsored... and that your share will come directly underneath with all other sign-ups coming under this share. Then, each month you and your networking contract can split a tasty sum. Just make sure that each of your letters to any CEO is accompanied by our standard L.A.N.T. SYSTEM™ brochure so that the CEO can get a good preliminary sense of what the System entails. To get this brochure and a sample of the cover letter you should send to your company CEO, contact Robert Blackman, Diversified Enterprises, P.O. Box 1390, Norman, OK 73070 (405) 360-9487. Once you know the CEO's appetite has been whetted, send Robert $10 and ask him to send out the entire L.A.N.T. SYSTEM™ kit, which explains in minute detail both how the System works... and how the company benefits. Once a CEO knows this, the chances he'll sign up his company — and that you'll make a very tidy fortune — are remarkably high. Have you ever heard of anything so intelligent... and so incredibly easy???

A Personal Note

It is clear to me that the network marketing universe is divided into two groups of people: those who understand the unparalleled power of leverage... and those who don't. For instance, take a fellow in my Ad-Net organization who contacted me recently about helping him build his primary MLM organization. I explained that if he really wanted to see rapid growth he'd turn the CEO of his primary MLM on to Ad-Net and sponsor the entire company. What I heard afterwards made me despair about the human condition.

He couldn't contact the CEO because...

- he didn't know him
- was sure his letter and follow-up phone call wouldn't be answered
- was really a "nobody", and besides
- he didn't have any stationery.

I kid you not!

This man, of course, is a lost cause. He's the kind of guy who's poor now (albeit 50-ish) and will always be poor. He doesn't want to know how to make his MLM business a success... and won't do what's necessary to help himself even when he's being spoon fed a winning proposition. I want you to know I feel complete and abiding contempt for such people; they disgust me. Making money in America is about organizing large groups of people and harnessing their purchasing power to your chariot. Leveraging allows you to do this. Sponsoring people at house parties and through warm marketing doesn't. Yet in the supposedly great bastion of capitalism, we have people supposedly trying to make money who won't do what's necessary to get the information they need and the system to do so.

To wit:

- maybe you don't know the CEO personally, but you're a member of his company. Like it or not, he's got to pay attention to you — if you persist.
- maybe your first letter and first phone call, and second letter and second phone call and even third letter and third phone call won't be answered. Just because something's valuable to the company doesn't mean the CEOs going to get it right away. Persist. It's what distinguishes the also-rans from the winners.
- as for the "self-esteem" issue, you're only a "nobody" if that's how you feel.
- as for the stationery. I believe they're still selling the stuff, right. (Personally, I haven't had business stationery ever since I got my computer. Where's the problem here... except that our would-be millionaire doesn't really want to bestir himself?)

Fortunately, there are other people who do get it. I like working with these people. When I explain leveraging to them, their eyes light up and I can see saliva glistening at the corners of their mouths. No wonder! The entire MLM concept is a leveraging concept... what I've just shared with you simply takes the concept further into ever more profitable developments. The question, therefore, isn't whether the system is profitable... the question, dear reader, is whether you have the brains to profit from it. *That* remains to be seen...

Last Words On Leads

There are, of course, still other ways of generating leads, including:

- list rental
- purchase "opportunity seeker" names, and
- reviewing ads in the opportunity press.

Each, however, offers significant problems. Let's look briefly at each.

▮ List Rental

There are two ways to use a rented list of name: to recruit by mail and to generate a lead.

▮ Recruitment by Mail

Recruitment by mail is very alluring to lots of people in network and opportunity marketing. It's easy to see why. All you have to do is:

- rent some names
- use the company's "tested" mailing piece
- pay for this piece and the postage, and
- sit back to await an avalanche of checks and positive responses.

On this basis, tens of thousands of people each year throw their money down the drain, never beginning to recoup more than a small fraction of what they've invested. Here's why.

- Poor name quality. Over the years I've come to be very suspicious, very suspicious indeed, about the quality of "hot" opportunity prospects. Personally, I had my worst experience in mail-order by trusting a broker who claimed to have such a list. The broker in question still gets in touch with me every once in a while attempting to solicit my business. But as I've told him, after I've taken a 7K hit from a company that's supposed to know about the quality of names (but clearly didn't), I'll be damned if I try that tainted "authority" again. So, beware!

  ▮ **Find out how the names were generated.** If by ads, see a copy of the ad.

  ▮ **Find out when the ad(s) ran.** Lists older than 90 days should be avoided whenever possible.

■ **Ask who else has recently used the file.** Contact one or two such people to find out how they've done. Remember, caution, caution, caution!

■ **Do the smallest possible test you can.** Most brokers want to rent you a minimum number of names, like 5,000. But 5,000 is too many for your first test. 1,000 will do nicely. If the broker still wants to charge you for 5,000, pay the difference but ask that it be applied to your next order. If you don't place another order because the first test was unsuccessful, it's a small price to pay for saving what it would actually have cost to produce and mail the remaining 4,000 pieces.

■ **Find out if the names have telephone numbers.** All too often the people who assemble opportunity lists don't bother with phone numbers. Why, just recently I was talking to the owner of a decent-sized company who was astonished when I asked for phone numbers. "We've never thought of collecting them," he confessed. Amazing! What this tells me is that he's got so many suckers quite prepared just to mail (and unprepared to do any follow up) that collecting phone numbers just doesn't make sense. Beware! You already know how important phone numbers are. You're not going to be able, of course, to call 1,000 people... but you can certainly call, say, 100 of them to attempt to bolster your solicitation. (Or, if you're really organized, you can co-op the leads and phone numbers to people in your organization. Each of 10 people ought to be able to call 100, if they're serious.)

■ **Monitor everything.** It's amazing to me how few people put a code on their mailing pieces and track everything that comes in. Don't be one of them! Code everything. And keep a file in your computer where you note responses, dates received, and business done.

■ **Expense.** No one needs to tell anyone who regularly uses the mail to solicit business that it's expensive to do so. Here's the budget for mailing 1000 of our very inexpensive self-mailers:

■ **Cost of 1,000 Staff of Life or Gourmet Coffee Club/Ad-Net self-mailers.** Imprinted 35.5 cents each plus $23.50 shipping.

(Keep in mind that the marketing communications produced by virtually all other companies are significantly more expensive than this; remember, they are in the printing business and derive a significant amount of revenue from selling you printing);

■ cost of affixing label, bundling and taking to post office – $230;

■ cost of bulk-rate postage for same (remember, in this case you'd need a bulk-rate permit which costs $75 per year).

■ cost of list rental for same – $75.

Total: $410.00

Now, let's say for the sake of discussion that you get a 1% response. That would be 10 responses.

If you were in a program which gave you a $30 sign-up bonus, you'd reap $300, not enough to cover your expenses. In this case, you're speculating that these people stay in the program a certain number of months and follow the recruiting guidelines to bring in people because, as you see, you actually lose money on the front-end.

As you can quickly see at a glance, mail-order recruitment just doesn't make economic sense, yet it's easy to see why so many people advocate it.

- The list broker makes money.

- The company and/or printer making available the marketing communication makes money.

- Even the post office makes money!

Actually, mail-order recruitment *may* make sense, but only if you have the means to cut your expenses.

- Do you have something you can swap for sensible opportunity lists? For instance, as you know I'm a card-deck publisher. I can swap cards in my deck and/or names that I have available in order to get leads. This significantly reduces the cost of any names I want. In short, I never pay full price. What about you?

- Do you have something you can swap for your printing requirements? Again, I do. I don't pay full-cost for my printing anymore. What about you?

- Are you prepared to do what's necessary to achieve maximum postal savings? I put all my mailings through a computer program that arranges for maximum savings. What about you? Or do you witlessly mail everything first class?

In short, think! Just because some self-serving yokel tells you you're going to be well off if you recruit by mail, do you really have what it takes to make money now — or in the near future?

■ *Lead-Generation By Mail*

Okay, you're now familiar with the hazards of outright recruitment by mail. What about lead-generation?

I know lots of people in the opportunity market who are keen to:

- rent you names

- sell you printing, and
- tell you that you can generate all the prospect leads you need if you send people a postcard and ask them to call you.

But is it true?

You already know what it costs to rent 1,000 names. (By the way, unscrupulous opportunity list brokers often attempt to charge lots more for list rental than the $50 per thousand cited above. Take heed!) If you'd like some good prospect lists at reasonable cost, call Robert Blackman at (405) 360-9487. We get new leads in every day.

To print 1,000 postcards costs $45 per thousand.

The postage for 1,000 postcards is $200.

Other expenses may include:
- the cost of using a copywriter to create the card
- two- or four-color processing for the card;
- the cost of a service to apply labels, bundle and take to post office.

It is easy to see why so many people advocate mail-order recruitment.

Let's look at some real numbers.

Say figuring in the factors above, the cost of mailing 1000 post-cards is between $235 – $500. Say that you get a 2% return. That is 20 people are willing to call and tell you that they're interested in learning more about the opportunity. Say that you're able to close 4 of these, or 20%. You're still in the hole!

In other words, it probably doesn't make any sense at all for you either to recruit by mail... or to try to generate leads by mailing a single post card to a rented list of prospects. It's just too expensive.

List Purchase

The same objections apply when someone is offering to let you buy a list. Ads with such offers are ubiquitous in the opportunity press. Once you respond to one (being a "hot" name yourself), you'll find that you'll be getting a lot of mail from others offering to rent or sell you names. I get such a solicitation nearly every day... and I pity the hapless people who have paid for my name. They've been completely mislead since all I do it toss their solicitation in the trash right away... just as I suspect the overwhelming majority of others do who receive it.

Reviewing Ads In The Opportunity Press

When you talk to people running opportunity ads of various kinds, they always complain that a large percentage of the responses they receive are from — people offering them yet another opportunity! This is revolting!

People running opportunity ads have the right to hear solely from serious people looking for a serious opportunity. They don't want to hear from those who have another opportunity to sell. Personally, I know that on any given ad 10% of the responses will be from those who want me to join them, instead of the other way around. By the same token, scarcely a day goes by when one of these people doesn't call or fax me, insistent that I pay attention to their opportunity.

IF THIS IS YOU, CUT IT OUT. AND MAKE SURE YOU DON'T EVER CONTACT ME!!!

Don't waste your time reading the ads in the opportunity press except to monitor new companies and your competition. And certainly don't insult the advertisers by insisting they pay attention to your opportunity when their first and only responsibility is doing what's necessary to develop theirs.

PLEASE!!!

Last Words On Prospect Lead Generating

I regard the ability to generate a continuing stream of prospect leads as one essential variable in becoming a success in any networking marketing or other opportunity. Unfortunately, I'm here to tell you that most people don't have a clue about generating leads and are often downright hostile when you try to instruct them in what they need to do.

In part, this is because they have heard for so long about the value of "warm marketing." But "warm marketing" for most people is not merely limiting; it's downright dangerous.

As we know, the vast majority of people in network marketing and other opportunities fail. Yes, over 95%. By the same token, the overwhelming majority of network marketing companies fail. As I write, of over 1,800 network marketing companies formed in the last few years, only TWENTY have reached their fifth year!

Now, link these unforgiving statistics to "warm marketing."

Say that like most people, you were all enthusiastic when you joined your network marketing company. Say that like most companies this one was a strong advocate of warm marketing. Say that as a result you started out, not by generating prospect leads as advocated in this chapter, but working on:

- your friends
- neighbors
- relatives
- colleagues and business associates, *etc.*

The theory of warm marketing is that these people will help you... whether they have any interest in the product/service or not. As a result, it is absolutely certain that you'll be able to sell product to and/or recruit some of these people into your organization.

What, then?

Well, the odds are that as soon as you've done this...

1) the company will fail. When only 20 out of 1,800 network marketing companies survive into their fifth year of business, you can be certain the odds are against your company prospering — not least because it has bet the ranch on "warm marketing." And when the company fails, the people who you've brought into the exercise are going to hold you responsible. I know. Years ago when I knew nothing about network marketing, I allowed myself to be recruited into one of the many diet companies then (and still) popping up. I knew the woman professionally who sponsored me; she was a trained dietitian and seemed to know what she was doing. However, the company was one of the 1,800 fatalities cited above... and when it collapsed (after so much hype), it soured my relationship with my acquaintance who avoided me thereafter. In fact, I've never spoken to her since. Multiply this common scenario by tens of thousands, and you see why network marketing has contributed so greatly to the destruction of probably millions of family and business relationships.

2) you'll run out of prospects. Everyone's "warm market" is limited. Even if you approach your aunts, uncles and cousins reckoned by the dozens you're still going to run out of prospects soon. What then? Well, either your business will start to decline (for the last day you recruit is the first day your business starts to atrophy), or you'll have to start scrambling for other alternatives. (Most people at this point make the fatal mistake of going into the kind of mail recruiting examined and condemned above.)

Thus, let me be very clear about this:

- "Warm marketing" is a sign not of marketing intelligence but of a bankruptcy in marketing intelligence. Companies that are based on "warm marketing" recruitment are companies that produce distributors with pitiable monthly incomes. After all, as it well known, the average Amway distributor makes well under $100 a month... and Amway is the quintessential "warm marketing" company. To be sure, there are people at the top in Amway who make many, many times this amount monthly... but their success comes at the cost of tens of thousands of distributors who have bought into a system that knowingly sacrifices them and ensures their infuriating lack of success.

Thus, run, don't walk away from a company that advocates recruitment primarily through "warm marketing."

- a company based on "warm marketing" techniques is a company that cannot attract the kinds of trained professionals that every successful network marketing opportunity needs. As you may know, I have a Ph.D. from Harvard; I know lots of other people who are as highly trained and who have secured top professional credentials from top educational institutions. Often these people are intrigued by network marketing. However, when they hear that they must recruit by "warm marketing" they lose their interest fast enough. What doctor, what lawyer, what accountant, what university professor or engineer seeking the benefits of leveraging for extra income can imagine himself going door to door signing up their friends and neighbors, selling toothpaste and diet powders from an over-the-shoulder bag? It's demeaning!!!

Companies relying on "warm marketing" ensure recruitment of the lowest grade opportunity seekers. Such people, with the obstinacy of the uneducated, think it's perfectly sensible... and indeed the only possible way... to peddle door to door. If you're a professional yourself you'll see immediately just how impossible this scenario is. Try to imagine yourself doing it! If you're not a trained professional, you must see it from the professional's standpoint because it is these trained professionals whom you want to recruit.

Day after day I encounter brain-washed people who have been imbued with the foolish belief that "warm marketing" is the only way to market an opportunity. THEY ARE WRONG.

- Companies advocate "warm marketing" because they haven't got a clue how to recruit and sustain independent distributors. A reliance on "warm marketing" by independent distributors is a sure sign that the company is bereft of useful marketing ideas for these crucial people;

- they don't give a thought to the lead-generation that is the necessary life's blood of any enterprise;

- because they make money the minute you sign up (enrollment fee) and from any initial purchases you are required to make, they don't care if you succeed or not. You have served your purpose just by signing up, and any other revenues you may generate are just icing on the cake.

- companies know that your friends and family will support you to a certain extent... and that, therefore, you will sell something through "warm marketing" thereby enabling you to mistakenly conclude that warm marketing works — all the while swelling the profits of the company.

- the companies rely on your greed and imprudence to blind you to their own lack of sustained independent distributor support and the short-comings of "warm marketing". Unfortunately, when they bet on some of your worst aspects, they're usually right!

Having said all this, you don't need to toss out "warm marketing" altogether. You just need to reconsider when you'll use it. While it shows very poor judgment to solicit your family, friends, neighbors, *etc.* before your network marketing program has proved itself... you'll do these people a favor by telling them about it once it has. In fact, at that point you probably won't even have to tell them... they'll be sniffing around, asking you. While prematurely soliciting those near and dear to you into something that so often ends so bitterly for so many is insane... to let these same people enjoy the benefits of a good thing once it has proved itself is a blessing. Thus, don't start with "warm marketing", but do include it once you start mining real gold.

Following this logic, I've succeeded in recruiting many thousands of people into my Staff of Life, Gourmet Coffee, and Ad-Net Success Teams WITHOUT USING ANY FORM OF WARM MARKETING. I reckoned that if I couldn't succeed without involving my friends and neighbors, then the venture wasn't worth entering in the first place. However, once I was sure things were working out, I put my sainted mother in all of the programs. At that time, I wrote her a note and told her that thereafter she'd be receiving small, but growing, monthly checks from the programs... and that all she had to do was cash them and shower maternal blessings on my comely head. She accepted my offering in the spirit in which it was meant, cashes the small (but, as predicted, growing) monthly checks... and wafts incense in my direction at regular intervals, telling all her friends (who have not, it seems, been gifted by children as solicitous as I am) of my bountiful, and regularly repeating, gift. My mother, bless her soul, hasn't a clue what the opportunities are or do; I don't ever intend to tell her either. But we're both happy all the same. This, dear friend is how you, too, should be using "warm marketing", and make no mistake.

CHAPTER 4

GETTING READY FOR THE RESPONSES

Have you ever responded to an opportunity ad, made a phone call — and never heard from the person at the other end? Have you ever mailed in a request for information and received nothing? OF COURSE YOU HAVE. It happens all the time.

Those marketing the opportunities will tell you, without batting an eye, that the information must have gotten lost in the mail... or that they never got the message. However, you know as well as I do that THEY'RE LYING. The truth is they're just bloody incompetent!

This chapter is here so you won't duplicate their sadly ineffectual efforts. Just as one absolute necessity of success in the opportunity business is generating a constant flow of leads, so another is handling these leads expeditiously.

To do this means thinking through how you'll respond before you have to respond, and making sure you've done everything possible so that you can respond without thought and with promptness. To achieve these desirable objectives, we'll review three basic situations:

- when people call you
- when people write you
- when you call people.

When People Call You

People calling you are your best prospects. That's why you should do everything possible to make sure they do. (For further information on this important subject, see my book NO MORE COLD CALLS: THE COMPLETE GUIDE TO GENERATING — AND CLOSING — ALL THE PROSPECTS YOU NEED TO BECOME A MULTI-MILLIONAIRE BY SELLING YOUR SERVICE.) Once they call, be sure you handle them properly — whether you're physically present or not.

▎ Answering Machine Message

With the best will in the world, you can't be physically available all the time to answer your phone. Even I, for instance, have been known to get out now and again for a breath of fresh air or, imagine, to get some sleep. Yet if you handle things properly, you're going to get prospect calls at these times... so, like a good Boy Scout, be prepared.

In this connection I think of a network marketing company I know where the switchboard closes at 5 p.m. and where the message they leave is entirely devoid of marketing thrust. It basically just says either leave a message or call back. Now, this is unimaginative — and futile.

You've got to be more with it than that.

What you need to do is turn your answering machine into a *prospecting* device. It must...

- provide a client-centered benefit and

- prime the prospect to leave all the information you need to make a preliminary decision about his bona fides as someone you should be investing your scarce resources in.

Does this kind of message work?

"Hello, this is Jane Doe. I'm not available right now. But your call is really important to me. Leave your name and number after the beep. Have a nice day."

Of course not. IT'S IDIOTIC.

Now try this:

"Hello, this is Jane Doe — your /name of company/ independent distributor. Let me show you the way to getting /the chief benefit offered by your company/. That's right, thousands of people around America are now profiting from this benefit — AND SO CAN YOU. Please leave your name and phone number after the beep. If you have network marketing experience, please tell me a little about it... let me know if you currently have people in your organization and how many and whether you are prepared — right now — to join our success team and profit from /chief benefit offered by your company./ Let me know when it's convenient for me to call and I'll be back in touch promptly."

See the difference?

The second message isn't just taking information from the prospect... it's asking for essential qualifying details. It seeks to discover not just that a prospect has called... but just how valuable the prospect is. If you get lots of messages like I do, who would you rather call first — a prospect with 50 people in his downline... or a prospect who just leaves his name and phone number and no qualifying details? Obvious, isn't it? Messages should gather details that allow you to prioritize and use your resources to best advantage.

Handling Messages

Just what you do once you get your message clearly indicates whether you're a marketer... or a fool. A marketer is prepared for all eventualities. He has thought through all the different alternatives and prepared for each. In short, his marketing is composed of two distinct parts: *planning* and *execution*. The planning takes place *before* any prospects appear... the execution is all he does *after* the prospects appear.

In this connection, the effective marketer is prepared for messages. He knows he's either going to work this lead himself... or refer it to a member of his organization. Let's look at both options.

▋ Handling The Lead Yourself

When you handle the lead personally, you've got to:

- store the data for future reference
- have available any personalized marketing communications
- have available your general marketing communications.

Clearly, a personal computer is essential here.

With your computer, you can:

- store the prospect data for easy use and retrieval;
- keep on file templates of all letters and other marketing communications which you can use and reuse for individual prospects.

Thus, think through in advance just how your computer can help and prepare yourself accordingly.

Your database, for instance, must contain:

- prospect name
- address
- phone
- fax
- date of first contact

I suggest, in fact, you have two databases:

1) the first should contain just the basic prospect information (above);

2) the second should contain notes of all contacts, their dates, your impressions, and information on the development of the relationship, what you've promised to do, when it was done, what remains to be done, *etc*.

The first database is purely factual; the second more impressionistic and action-oriented.

The second way a computer can help is by storing all your template marketing communications. Here you've got to think through everything that can happen with a phone prospect and prepare the appropriate documents accordingly:

- the prospect can ask for general information;
- the prospect can request particular information that you can supply;
- the prospect can request particular information that you cannot supply.

You need an appropriate template for each.

■ The Prospect Asks For General Information

When the prospect is calling in response, say, to one of your ads, he/she is probably just requesting general information. If your general information is available in self-mailer or other handy format (as it should be), this communication can be quite short.

- thanks for your inquiry about /name of your company/. I'm glad to supply the information you need.
- here are the chief benefits of joining (list them)
- here's all you have to do to join (namely, complete enclosed application/s)
- here's what I'm going to do to follow up (call in five business days, *etc.*)

It goes without saying that this material should be sent THE SAME DAY THE PROSPECT CONTACTS YOU!!!

■ The Prospect Requests Particular Information You Can Supply

From time to time, prospects call with quite specific questions. Perhaps they've looked at the program before and want to know what's happened since. Perhaps they have a friend in the program but want to have clarification on some point or other. It happens all the time. Be prepared!!!

In this template communication, say:

- thank you for your inquiry about /nature of inquiry/
- here's the information you require /provide it/
- I hope having provided you with this information that you will join /name of program/ and reap /major benefits of joining/
- I'll be calling you in five business days to follow up, and trust you will at that time join my organization.

Note: the thrust of all these documents is upbeat, positive, pro-active, leading. You're saying at all times: I'm giving you what you want. Now, you do what you need to do so that we can join forces and get you on my team. Remember, you are NOT in the information dissemination business. You're in the business of recruiting people as quickly as possible and making them full-fledged members of your team.

■ The Prospect Requests Particular Information You Cannot Supply

No matter how knowledgeable you are about your program, there's certain to come a time when some prospect poses a stumper. Don't fret. Get ready. Towards this end, either enlist the services of your upline sponsor, or, better, the most knowledgeable executive at the company's headquarters. In my Staff of Life organization, for instance, you already know we rely on Don Smyth, CEO. When I don't know the answer to a question, I refer the query to him for handling. And I so notify the prospect, thus:

- Thank you for your query about /nature of query/

- For an answer to this question, please refer to /name of your contact, title if any/ at /phone of contact/. He/she is in the best position to assist you.

- If I can be of any further assistance, please let me know.

Note: If you're *really* organized and have the kind of top-flight technical assistance I think necessary and demand for my own organization, you won't stop simply by sending this letter off by mail. No way! You'll fax a copy of this letter to your information contact and ask him/her to follow up promptly. It never ceases to astonish and favorably impress prospects when their query results in this kind of professional follow-up, now so rare in business, whatever the business. This kind of professionalism will go far towards recruiting new people into your group, so use it!!!

A Plea

As I've already said, when you're running an effective recruiting machine, your goal should always be to answer such queries the day you receive them. With your computer, printer and fax properly integrated into your office routine, there's absolutely no reason why this can't happen. I am constantly appalled by people who take weeks to follow up leads... as even, I regret to say, some dimmer-witted members of my own success teams occasionally sheepishly confess. I never let this slackness pass as acceptable, and if I ever find out that you're engaging in such poor practices, I'll whip your posterior, too.

Of course, you cannot answer these queries promptly if you don't have the supplies to do so. Thus, make sure that you always have on hand adequate supplies of:

- laser printer paper

- self-mailers and other marketing communications

- manila envelopes and other shipping materials
- suitable postage denominations.

One of the things that I find most irritating is how lax people are about maintaining proper amounts of necessary supplies. They forget that suppliers can't always make instant shipments when they're low. Here are some tips:

- if we have prepared your self-mailers through Diversified Enterprises, allow at least three weeks for imprinting your information and shipping. Thus, when you're down to a four-week supply of self-mailers, that's the moment to place your order. It's outrageous when people let their supplies dwindle to a few days and then rant and rave because it takes the usual amount of time to get their order out. Prepare in advance!

- if you have your stationery supplies delivered (as I do), work with one account representative only. Make sure he knows what you need to order... make sure he explains the company's order procedures to you thoroughly. Then make sure you follow them. Find out if the supplies you want are regularly kept on hand or have to be specially ordered... and if they must be specially ordered just how long it takes. In short, think through your needs... and work directly with the supplier to make sure you know just how long it takes to get what you require.

Resource

If you're going to succeed in network marketing, there are certain tools you must have, including:

- a low-cost long-distance service
- personal computer
- letter-quality printer
- fax.

Note: To lower your phone bill, give me a call to check out the details on our discount phone service. You'll find our rates very competitive. On outbound calls, your cost is only 15 cents per minute during the day, 14 cents in the evening, billed in 6 second increments. And our 800# service is only 15 cents per minute in the day and 16 cents in the evening. 85% of Americans are still overpaying their monthly phone bill. Don't know if you're one of them? Do this quick check: pull out a copy of last month's phone bill. Divide the total long distance and 800# charges by the total number of minutes. If you're paying more than our prices quoted above, you're giving money to the phone company! Switch to our service today!

A Tip

Since you're going to be mailing a lot, check to see if your post office accepts MasterCard/VISA. If so, get one of the credit cards that rewards every dollar you spend on it with some kind of additional benefit. For example, I have one through Continental Airlines that provides me with one frequent flyer mile for every dollar I charge on the card. In this way, I've built up an unbelievable reserve of free trips, largely subsidized by trips to the post office. This benefit makes the fact you're spending so much money on stamps, office equipment, office supplies, *etc.* just that much more bearable. One small point, however. Pay off the amount owed on the card when you get your statement each month. The reason? Cards with these kinds of travel and other benefits charge a much higher interest rate than other credit cards you can get these days. If you use the card and pay off your balance promptly, you get a nice free benefit. On the other hand, if you're financing at 18%, it's just not worth the price.

▮ Referring The Lead

As your organization develops and your lead-generating vehicles produce more and more prospects, you're just not going to have time to handle all the leads yourself. Besides, it's counter-productive to do so. You WANT to refer leads to people in your organization. You WANT them to work an increasing percentage of the leads... so that your organization grows larger still. So, be prepared!

The original referral. *Courtesy of Michaelangelo.*

First, develop a template like the following:

WHAT HAVE YOU DONE TODAY TO RECRUIT AT LEAST ONE PERSON INTO YOUR ORGANIZATION? REMEMBER, FOLLOW THE "AWESOME POWER OF ONE" SYSTEM TO DOUBLE THE SIZE OF YOUR ORGANIZATION EVERY MONTH!!!

your company name

address

phone

fax

date

To: /name of independent distributor in your organization/

From: /your name/

Following contacted me today to get <specific information on your opportunity.>

prospect name

address

day phone

evening phone

fax

I informed this prospect that you would be sending <whatever you're sending> and would follow up five business days later. I also provided the prospect with your name and phone number in case he/she wishes to contact you directly.

<Add here any specific comments about prospect or directions for distributor. Such information may include previous network marketing experience, number of people in downline, available resources, constraints or limitations, *etc*. In short, provide what will help your distributor understand this prospect and make the best possible presentation.>

Notes on Closing & Organizational Development

1) Do what's necessary TODAY to close this prospect. This means sending necessary information, or calling or following up TODAY as appropriate.

2) If this person has called me (as noted above), he/she is already qualified. <Note: this means that you should always be qualifying phone-in leads.> Otherwise, you must call to pre-qualify. Don't just send information out; make sure the prospect is a real prospect before making any investment.

3) When you talk to your prospect, ask him/her right away whether he/she is ready to join <name of your opportunity.> Remember, people do join just because you ask them. If your prospects are ready to join, get them to complete the necessary paperwork when you're on the phone. Then tell them what's necessary for them to get started (i.e. join our co-op prospect lead generating program, join Ad-Net, purchase self-mailers and other marketing communications, *etc*.) Make sure the prospect has all the relevant information he/she needs to move ahead.

4) If prospect isn't ready to join now, find out why. If the prospect has questions you can answer, answer them directly. If you cannot answer the prospect's questions, tell the prospect you'll get the information and schedule a time when you can get back to the prospect with it. At that point, present the information and ask the prospect to join.

5) If the prospect needs time to "think about it," ask why. Is there something you can do RIGHT NOW to expedite the close? If so, act accordingly. If not, find out how much time the prospect needs and follow up accordingly. Remember, it is your job to keep control of the sales sequence.

6) If you follow up again and the prospect still won't join, ask why. Be sure that you know what's keeping the prospect from joining. Ask whether if the prospect's concerns/questions are dealt with, he/she will join. Keep pushing for the close. Say, "What will it take for us to do business today?", or "What will it take for you to join today?" If you're not getting a good, solid, believable answer, say so, and, if necessary, ring off pleasantly to go to a more productive prospect. Otherwise, keep doing what's necessary to close.

7) Make sure your new recruit understands "The Awesome Power of One" system and will work to bring in at least one new person each month and assist his/her downline members do the same.

A few comments about this form:

- This template is designed for easy faxing. It's just one-page long.

- Personally, I like to start off with a goal for the independent distributor — in this case, doing what's necessary to achieve my top rank in the company.

- make sure that your follow-up information is on the form and the date of this transaction.

- Include detailed comments about the prospect whenever possible.

- Provide step-by-step guidelines about how to follow this prospect up for best results. Never be afraid of saying, "FOLLOW UP TODAY." You'd be amazed at just how many people procrastinate about following up leads. It's disgusting...

- Don't hesitate to ask the distributor to get back to you with a progress report. This is a way of your staying on top not only of what happens to this particular prospect... but of checking the overall progress of your distributor and making helpful suggestions on how to improve performance.

Last Comments About Phoned-In Leads When You Are Not Available

Occasionally, despite your explicit directions to a phoned-in prospect, this prospect will not leave complete details. Here's what you should do in this case:

- if the prospect doesn't leave a phone number. This person is NOT a good prospect, whatever he may say. People looking for opportunities KNOW they're to leave phone numbers. When they don't, it's because they're just window shopping. I regard them as very poor prospects. In times past, I have had a template letter for such people saying:

    – I've received your request for information on /name of opportunity/

    – This is a wise decision on your part, especially since /name of opportunity/ offers the following compelling benefits /list them/.

    – Unfortunately, I cannot supply your information without a phone number for follow up. Please provide by calling /phone number/ or fax information to /fax number./

    – I'll be happy to supply you with the details you request after I hear from you again.

I say I *used* to have such a template. Now, I get just too many leads to trouble with the unhelpful people who can't be bothered to follow directions. What I do now is simply add their name/address to my general catalog mailing list. I do not refer the lead to anyone since a lead without a phone number is a very weak lead, indeed. If the party wishes to respond to the opportunity details in my catalog, he can. If not, well, it's our mutual loss.

If you do not maintain a mailing list, then I suggest you send a version of my template letter requesting further details. But so you won't be tormented by this uncooperative individual, send the letter, then toss the "prospect" information. Without the phone number, it's of no further use to you.

- if the prospect asks that you either fax your information or send via an overnight or faster-than-usual delivery service. If the prospect has not left a phone number, proceed as above. If he has, call to further qualify. Lots of people get a thrill by demanding instant service... when they have absolutely no intention of following through promptly. I know. I always send my materials out by regular mail. No one really needs to make an opportunity decision in 24 hours, no matter how self-important they seem. The one and only time I broke this rule was when one creature who thinks he's God's gift to networking insistently demanded that I send some opportunity materials to him via overnight delivery since he assured me he was making a decision about which oppportunity to join right away. I didn't know the man then, didn't know that having other people jump up upon demand is his one and only specialty. I sent the materials he wanted overnight... but only after securing his assurance that he'd get back to me at a particular time with a decision. It goes without saying that this egotistical and unprofessional guy, one of the legion of self-proclaimed network marketing guru's, never bothered to meet his obligation. Having gotten me to jump... he relapsed into his usual, desultory, self-defeating habits. When I in turn insisted that he meet his obligation to me, the man responded by sending me a series of the most ridiculous letters I've ever seen... instead of saying "Yes, I'll join," or "No, I won't join," he sent me letter after letter (most faxed in the middle of the night proving that at least for poison pen letters the verbose, pompous ass keeps the midnight oil burning) providing voluminous details on:

- the square footage of every office he'd ever rented;

- just where all his bank accounts had been since he was a teen-ager;

- all the important people he'd known in his life (his four-star list even included his encounter with some European *horse trainer*... as if this fact qualified him to be recognized as a network marketing authority — amazing!!!);

- the papers he'd written (none recently, by the way);

- the people he'd studied with in graduate school thirty years ago....

... all designed to prove beyond contention what a superior person he undoubtedly was.

I was angry, of course, when I first started getting these letters. Then I realized this creep was an egomaniac of no mean proportions, a man who delighted in giving orders... not in working with people to help them achieve success, and certainly not a man in whose word any reliance could be put. So, in short order, I started laughing at his letters — all of which I kept — knowing that God had provided me in this maniac with the perfect anecdote for my next book... and so it has proved.

Unfortunately, you, too, are just as likely to encounter losers as superbly insistent, demanding, unhelpful and self-centered as the one who soiled my life... so learn to rely on your first, instinctive reactions. Question this person closely as to his intentions... then mail the information he needs unless he's willing to supply you with his own Federal Express account number. Qualifying early will mean you won't have the adulterated pleasure I enjoyed of receiving the midnight messages of an MLM madman. (By the way, someone suggested after reviewing the guy's correspondence that he was probably sexually obsessed with me. It's just a hypothesis... what do you think? Or do you think he's just frustrated that someone beside himself is getting the ink in the industry these days?)

When You're Available To Handle The Called-In Prospect Lead

The game gets more interesting and faster-paced when you're available to handle the called-in prospect lead yourself. Again, you've got to be prepared to handle this situation for your utmost advantage.

- Start by getting the basic prospect information, name, address, phone.

- Then start the crucial qualifying process.

- Ask if the prospect knows what network marketing is.

- Ask if he/she has had success in it previously. (Your ideal candidate is someone who's been in network marketing before, knows the ropes, has successfully built another organization and is seriously looking for a new opportunity. These people are like gold... and should be treasured accordingly. Your job is to find out if this is the kind of person you're speaking to.)

- Ask what the prospect really needs to know to make a decision. (Different people have different needs. It's not your job to launch into some kind of canned sales presentation. It *is* your responsibility to discover just what the prospect needs to be able to sign up now... and to do what's necessary to meet these reasonable needs.)

- Ask if the prospect has the resources to commit to building a profitable organization. No organization can be built on air alone. Everyone needs resources to build a business, whatever the business. Network marketing is no exception, although people try all the time to delude themselves into thinking otherwise. If the person tells you he has no money, no time, no willingness to succeed, no desire to commit (even if he doesn't come out so baldly and say these things... but that you must discern them through all the words he spews), run, don't walk in the opposite direction! You're dealing with a time-waster, and you just can't afford that.

Note: As you can see, it's not your job just to take down basic information about the prospect and ask if he'd like your "literature". Any trained monkey can do that. If you focus just on getting this information, you're not working properly. It's also not your job to let the prospect control the discussion. Remember, the more successful your group is, the more you've got to direct questions to the prospect and elicit information from the prospect. You want to qualify the prospect, to ensure that he's just the right kind of person for your organization. Of course, I know this is more difficult at the beginning. When you have no one in your organization and no evidence of current success, it's hard to act successful — but this is precisely the moment when you must do so, when you must keep control of the conversation, when you must do everything you can to qualify your prospect. After all, when you're not successful, resources are at their most limited — time, money, even your personal resolve. That's why you must do everything to ensure that the person you're talking to is serious. Put the onus of proving this seriousness on the *prospect*. It is never your responsibility to work with people who won't provide this evidence. And it is never sensible to proceed if you have the slightest suspicion that the person you're dealing with just won't work as part of your success team.

The hardest lesson for new people in network marketing to learn is that they are not on trial... the prospect is. So long as you are willing to do everything you need to do to ensure success, it's your bounden duty to ensure that the prospect will do everything that needs to be done to ensure success, too. Bending over backwards for someone merely because they express casual interest is just plain dumb. Probe. Find out. Learn. Prod. Then act on what you discover... whether that action is for the legitimate dispatch of marketing materials overnight... or hanging up the phone and terminating this "prospect" forever.

If you're just starting out, it's a good idea to write down all your qualifying questions and put them near the phone for easy access. Personally, I work at a computer station where I can grab the phone on the first ring. While the person is telling me why he's calling (identifying himself as a prospect), I can easily call up the screen with all the qualifying questions on it, thereby being certain I won't miss anything important. Alternately, you can copy these questions into a new file and simply record the information as you get it. Don't try to rely on your memory for anything. I have a very good memory, but I wouldn't trust it for a minute when it comes to keeping track of crucial prospect data.

Analyze Not Only What The Prospect Says, But How He Says It

Your job during this conversation is to assess this person, to see if he's a real prospect, or just a time-waster. Your ability to do this expeditiously is vitally important. Of course, you're going to listen carefully to what the prospect says.

- Are his answers real, believable?

- Is he willing to be candid with you about his situation and expectations?

- Does he ask you good questions about your organization, how you work, and about what you expect from him?

Real prospects get serious quickly. They don't want to waste their time; they want to know if you know what you're doing. They're willing to both answer your direct questions... and ask some of their own to find out.

Other, more subtle signs will also help:

- Do you get the feeling the person is leveling with you? If the person won't talk to you directly now, he's probably not a good prospect.

- Is the prospect trying to be helpful... or do you get the feeling he's being defensive, trying to protect himself?

- Do you get the sense that this is just another big talker, or someone who understands that making money is not a lark in the park... but the result of a carefully considered, and daily implemented, *process*?

Remember, you are under no obligation whatsoever to deal with anyone whom you feel is not a real prospect. You are NOT in the business of merely sending out "information." You are not in the business of catering to the whims of people who aren't serious and who won't do what's necessary to show you that they'd make a suitable addition to your team. Your job is plain: to do everything possible until you are reasonably certain you're dealing with someone who's really going to give your opportunity serious consideration. If you don't feel this way, finish pleasantly and go on to the next prospect.

What To Do When You've Discovered A Real Prospect

Real prospects like structure. They want you to know what you're doing... and they want you to provide leadership and structure. Don't blow it!

- Before the conversation ends, make sure you've asked the person in question to tell you that he's a real prospect. Say something like, "I've enjoyed our conversation and found it productive. It seems to me you really are a prospect for a solid network marketing opportunity. Would you confirm this for me so we can go on to the next step?" **Note**: if the person won't confirm his prospect status at this point, he's probably *not* a prospect, and you should proceed accordingly.

- Once you've received the confirmation from the prospect that he is indeed a prospect, tell him what happens next — what you'll be sending, when you'll be sending it, what you'd like the prospect to do, when you'll be following up. It's not the prospect's job to be familiar with your procedures. It's yours. Unfortunately, this kind of clarity is all too often missing in prospect conversations. Too often marketers are simply grateful to have got through the call without tripping over themselves that they forget that the call is only an *element* of a successful sales sequence. You've got to get through this call successfully, of course, but as soon as you've determined that the person is indeed a prospect, you've got to be planning your next moves... moves which lead to the recruitment of this person into your organization.

Note: we Americans are in a period in our history where we're maddeningly irresponsible about commitments we've undertaken. People think nothing of making appointments and not only not keeping them... but not bothering to tell anyone they've changed their minds. Indeed, we've reached such a nadir in this country in terms of professional relations that the people behaving so irresponsibly are actually strongly put out if anyone dares to challenge them on the point. "Don't cha know it's your right to behave as irresponsibly as you want?", they seem to say.

Nowhere is this form of self-destructive behavior more evident than in the ranks of opportunity seekers. Perhaps because so many of these people are poorly educated, not well off, and the product of inferior backgrounds and limited present circumstances, opportunity seekers see nothing wrong in telling you one thing... all the while intending to do something else. Such behavior, of course, is the mark of a cad... but such caddishness now seems entirely acceptable in American business. Well, friend, resolve that you will be part of the solution, not part of the problem.

When you make a follow-up appointment with your prospect, make sure he writes down the time; make sure you do, too! Indicate that you'll be calling promptly at that time, and that you need to know well beforehand if the prospect can't keep the appointment. Before you finish the call, confirm the time once more.

If You're Ridiculously Well Organized

The prospect you've now gone so far to qualify is like gold, and should be treated as such. To this end, create a template document in your computer that confirms what you're doing and what happens next, thus:

- Thank the person for speaking with you. If he's approached the matter of your opportunity with seriousness, he deserves your thanks and respect for he has given you something he can never reclaim: namely his time.

- Confirm when you'll be following up.

- Take this opportunity to again stress the major benefits of your opportunity. Keep hitting these benefits over and over again... until the prospect really gets them.

When People Write You

Another way people will contact you is either by mail or fax. As always, you must be prepared. In writing this section, I think of someone I know who recently took a business opportunity card in a card-deck. Although warned about the number of leads he and his wife could expect and the speed with which they'd come in, these know-it-alls failed to pay attention. As a result, nothing was ready when their responses came in. Thus, when they should have been attending to the crucial business of qualifying and closing, what they were doing instead was running around getting their marketing communications ready. Since this ended up taking lots longer than they expected, their leads didn't get dealt with for over 60 days... by which time, of course, most of the people who'd requested information had forgotten they'd ever done so. Stupid.

So that this can never happen to you, follow these guidelines:

- Be prepared to respond to your leads within 24 hours. This means making sure you've got everything you need ready to go, including:

  ▌ marketing communications/self-mailers

  ▌ reply materials like envelopes

  ▌ telephone qualifying script

  ▌ follow up cover letter, *etc.*

Your recruiting effort divides into just two parts — planning and execution. *Before* you get any leads, you *plan*. This means thinking through precisely what you're going to need and doing all the necessary work to ensure that when the lead actually comes in all you have to do is execute... not think. Unfortunately, this is precisely what most people don't do. They don't think ahead... and thus, when the lead appears, they are left scrambling to determine a suitable course of action. Not surprisingly, the lead can hardly be expected to find such lack of preparation enthralling, and thus he goes elsewhere... while you're still trying to figure out what to do.

Idiotic!

Rule 1, then: prompt response is crucial.

- Determine all the means you'll use to respond. These responses include...

    —putting a lead co-op together. As you surely must have glimpsed by now, I am a big advocate of putting lead co-ops together. Many distributors have very limited marketing budgets. They can't afford to purchase 50,000 or 100,000 card-deck cards, for instance, from their own resources. Fair enough. But *all* people can organize co-ops... where people purchase a share of the leads for a reasonable cost of between $1-$2 per lead. If you've followed the directions in this resource (and if not, you should be ashamed of yourself), you've organized a co-op and are prepared to disperse the leads accordingly, ordinarily by mail.

    —you may also fax selected leads to your distributors, particularly if they're local or have let you know they need leads promptly.

    —you can also, of course, get on the phone and qualify some or all of the leads yourself.

Here's what you need for each alternative.

■ Co-op

If you've decided to assemble a co-op you need:

- the names and addresses of all participants in the co-op
- the number of shares (or leads) they purchased, and
- a sheet of directions on how to work the leads you're sending. As previously pointed out, do not assume that people know how to work leads. It would be ideal, of course, if all members of your organization read this resource. *That* would really help your lead-closing percentage!

■ Fax

The same applies if you are faxing leads. Never just fax leads... always fax guidelines on how to work the leads along with the leads themselves. The clearer you are with your distributor about what he has to do and when he should do it, the better for all concerned.

■ Phone Follow-Up

The wildly erroneous assumption exists that just because someone has mailed in a lead, you don't have to qualify the lead. This is ridiculous. A mailed-in lead is the *beginning* of a sequence which will either result in the prospect becoming one of your distributors... or ending up in the trash. When you see a mailed-in response you're not going to know which alternative is likely to happen. You are not, after all, clairvoyant. That's why you need to pre-qualify… and why, again, working leads through a co-op makes sense.

Say you purchased even 50,000 cards in my card-deck for your opportunity. In 30-45 days you'd receive between 250-750 leads, an enormous number to work unless you were available full time and were resolved to make such a major commitment of time and resources. Instead of trying to work them all yourself, get smart. Involve others. In my deck 50,000 cards cost just $750. Thus, you can involve 10 people for just $75 each, a trifling sum. Say that 500 leads come in, a reasonable 1% response. Each person would get about 45 leads. Now, you will notice that 45 is not 10% of 500. That's because I've figured things so that you get 1/11 of the leads for free, a kind of commission on the deal.

Because of the way the leads would come in from a card-deck, you'd probably end up dispersing them something like this:

- week 2 after the card deck drops, one lead mailing to people in your co-op;
- week 3 two mailings
- week 4 two mailings
- week 5, one mailing
- week 7, one mailing.

In other words as the response peaks, you'd mail leads more often, reducing the mailings as the response drops again.

There's a considerable benefit to arranging things like this: your co-op participants get their leads in easy batches, rather than all at once. I've discovered in practice that sending 50 leads to someone who's not experienced in the business is a big mistake. It's just too many for them to work with effectively. Instead, it's better to send between 10-20. After all, remember what your co-op members have to do with their leads:

- call to pre-qualify them, to ensure that they arc real prospects;
- send marketing communications to those who are real prospects;
- schedule follow-up calls;
- keep the appointments;
- start new recruits off in the business, *etc.*

Yes, sending not more than 20 leads at a time makes sense.

Note: if you're like me and you enter all the leads in a computer database for further follow up, handle data entry as soon as possible in the day. Then divide the leads among people in your organization and mail promptly.

Another Note: try whenever possible to assign leads to people in their local area or in some other logical way. Thus, give all the Ohio leads to people in Ohio... and let women work on their female counterparts, *etc*. It's always easier for like to work with like. Assigning prospect leads in this fashion makes it easier for your distributors.

When You Call People

So far we've been discussing what happens when people call you... when people write you. Now it's time to deal with what happens next... when it's time for you to follow up. Please note, I am NOT saying when you make cold calls. I don't approve of cold calls. I despise them. I don't make them. And I cannot advise you to make them either. The entire thrust of this resource is on how to get people to contact you... and what to do then.

I'm always astonished when I hear from people selling opportunities who just get on the phone and call me cold. Invariably, I give them short shrift. Why not? I didn't ask them into my life. I didn't give them leave to approach me, to waste any of my time. I don't want the "benefits" they're offering... I don't even want to hear the shortest presentation on why my life is going to be better off because of them. <**Note**: just in case you thought, after reading this book, that you'd bring your opportunity to my attention, expecting me to hear you out politely and scrutinize your offering with careful consideration, think again. My partner Robert Blackman & I do, of course, review and join new opportunities. But only after the CEO of the company is familiar with our L.A.N.T. System and this book!>

So, I'm most decidedly *not* talking about making cold calls. I'm talking instead of how to use the phone to follow up people you have already decided are qualified.

Note: you'll notice I am advocating use of the phone for follow-up instead of face-to-face meetings. This is because I regard such meetings ordinarily as a complete waste of time. I have built three very large organizations in The Staff of Life, Gourmet Coffee Club, and Ad-Net with virtually no such meetings. And it would be with absolutely no such meetings except that I gave way a year or so ago at the urgent request of a prospect who insisted on seeing me. When he got here, I discovered that seeing him was a giant waste of time; that he was unprepared. Even though he did sign up into one of my organizations, he has never done anything since, despite much prodding. He gave me a lot of humanist crap about why he needed to see me to get motivated, *etc*. Even though I didn't buy it then, I succumbed and made the appointment. But it would have been far wiser to adhere to my usual policy. Take heed!

Here's how to handle the follow-up:

- Call when you said you were going to. If you can't keep the appointment, call as soon as you know you can't and arrange another one. If you can't connect directly with your prospect, leave a detailed message on his answering machine indicating your inability to keep the appointment and provide two convenient alternatives to reschedule. Ask him to call you back ASAP. (Good prospects will be happy to return this call and by returning it, they clearly indicate they are worthy of your consideration.)

- If you connect with your prospect, ask him right off if he's ready to join your program. All possibilities occur in marketing, and this includes immediate sign-up. Indeed, once you get into the swing of the kind of marketing advocated in this resource, you'll find that people will call you and *ask* to sign up, that you will not have to make any sales presentation at all. If this hasn't happened to you yet, it will, because when you are promoting a client-centered marketing approach this kind of easy sign-up happens.

- If the prospect is not ready to sign up right away, ask whether he thinks yours is a program of value in which he can make money. If the prospect feels that you are offering value and that he can make money in your program, the odds are very good that you'll sponsor him... after handling his questions.

- If the prospect says he's not sure your program offers value and that he can make money in it, ask why. At this point, untrained marketers pull back, fearing any kind of "confrontation." But as I can tell you, ask 100 people their opinion about anything, and you're very like to get 100 different answers. Even if you were offering the best program in the world, there would still be people (often irredeemably ignorant people to be sure) who'd find something wrong with it. It's your responsibility to find out if you're dealing with a reasonable objection or with something that the prospect is using as a cover-up for something else (like lack of money) as so often happens.

Note: part of being prepared for these conversations is knowing what kinds of things the prospects are likely to say and having your considered response available at your fingertips. Unfortunately, the network marketing companies are of virtually no assistance here. It is the job of *every* director of marketing at *every* network marketing company to brainstorm a list of the 25 top objections to joining the company and then to craft compelling responses. Sadly, no MLM marketing director seems to see his job in this fashion. Instead, they're ordinarily as witless as one woman director of marketing I talked to while writing this resource who told me she'd never stoop to creating such a useful marketing communication. Why? "Because we don't like to interfere with our entrepreneurs. We like them to figure things out for themselves." This woman ought to be shot. An opinion like this clearly indicates that she not only knows nothing about marketing but doesn't care a fig either for the interests of the company or the lives of the independent distributors who are the essential foundation of the company. If I ran an MLM company, the first thing I'd do is throw this woman into the field and let her sink or swim by her own precepts and see just how much she liked it. I trust God takes notice of this humble aspiration...

- Since your company hasn't done the work it's supposed to, if you're going to make a success of your involvement in it, you're going to have to do the work yourself. This means creating an "objections" file in your computer software. As you either think of or hear objections from prospects, promptly record them. The first time you hear an objection, your response to it may not be of Noble Prize quality. Don't worry. If you really don't know the answer, say, "I'll be happy to get the answer to that point and get back to you." There's absolutely nothing wrong with not knowing everything, particularly when you're new in the company. Indeed, even when you're not. I don't know everything there is to know about all the companies I'm involved with, but I know how to find out. This is where upline support and company liaisons come in. By all means admit you don't know the answer, then do what's necessary to get it... so long as you think the question reasonable and the answer crucial to recruiting your prospect. By the way, make sure to ask the prospect whether he'll join if the answer to his question is satisfactory.

Note: once you've got a good answer to the objection, record that, too. Don't assume you're going to remember the best way of answering an objection. Trusting your memory is a good way to get things wrong. Instead, log the objections and the responses. And be sure to upgrade your responses as you learn more about your program and become more skillful in presenting it.

Another Note: to get you started, here are some characteristic objections you're likely to hear and must, therefore, prepare for:

- "Your program costs too much." Your response should show why your program actually isn't a cost, but an investment. How will the prospect save money through your program; what benefits will he get from the program he can't get elsewhere? Drive this point home, since you'll find this a crucial objection.

- "Your company is new (and there untried)." Point to the experience level of the people who founded the company. Yes, the company may be new but the people behind it have some kind of experience. Point out, too, why your company is a solid advance on other, more established companies.

- "Your company is old (and therefore opportunity is limited)." Point out just how much opportunity remains. Point to the benefit of an established track record.

- "I don't think I can make any money with your program." You have to know precisely how money is made in your company and must be able to show your prospects how to do so. Point to your marketing program. Show how complete and easy it is. Remember, if you don't master this point, you'll never succeed in network marketing.

- "I don't have any time." Point out all the ways you and/or your company have available to save time. Do you produce self-mailers that the prospect only needs to address? Do you generate leads for the prospect and send them directly to him? Do you offer telemarketing support? In short, stress all the ways available of saving time. (**Note**: if you're having a hard time on this point, as you will with many network marketing opportunities, you'd better tell your company CEO right away about The L.A.N.T. SYSTEM™. Our system is so thorough that all the independent distributor has to do to make money is address a self-mailer and lick a stamp. Can you say as much for your program???)

- "I'm terrible on the phone." I'd guess that 99% of independent distributors hate the phone. That's one reason why so many fall so easily into the "recruit-by-mail" trap. Do you provide a telemarketing script? Upline telephone assistance, or, as with Tele-Close, professional telemarketing support? If so, say so... since dealing with your prospects' fear of the phone will improve your recruiting dramatically.

- "I only want to work in my neighborhood." Many prospects (as well as lots of independent distributors themselves) have the absolutely insane idea of working only within a few short blocks of their homes. THIS IS RIDICULOUS. We live in the age when every smart person is doing everything he can to develop broader, more universal markets. That, after all, is what the North American Free Trade Agreement (NAFTA) is all about. Don't fly in the face of this trend... use it. Point out that recruiting nationally or internationally (the way we do in my programs) is the way to go and show the ways you have to assist this recruitment. Personally, whenever I hear the "I only want to work locally" excuse, I fume inwardly because of its shear stupidity. Maybe you'll be calmer than I am when you hear it but, like me, you've got to turn this person around to join the 20th century!

Note: within a short time, you'll have heard virtually all the objections you're ever going to hear. It's been months now since I've heard anything new. After about 60 days in your opportunity, take your "objections list" and circulate it for editorial improvement. Send copies to your upline support, the director of marketing at your company, and the independent distributors under you who show the most promise or who have already demonstrated recruiting ability. Ask them to add additional objections and to edit the responses. Then take the best of what you've got and rework the objection responses. After you've done this, circulate this information to all members of your organization. Put a circled C (©) on it with the date, thus indicating it's covered by copyright. You don't want everyone in the company — or the company itself — to use this, after all. It's your brainchild, yet another benefit of using this resource!

Moving Towards The Close

Your job when soliciting prospects is to isolate their objections and polish them off, one by one. The opening of your conversation should go something like this,

You: Hello, Mr. Prospect, this is /your name/. I'm calling for the appointment we scheduled last week, to recruit you into /name of your opportunity./ Is this a convenient time to talk?

Prospect: Yes, it is.

(If the prospect says it isn't, reschedule the appointment.)

You: Did you receive the marketing material on /name of company/ and did you have the chance to review it?

Prospect: Yes, I did.

(If the prospect says he didn't receive the material and it has been more than five business days since you sent it the first time, wait three more days and then check with the prospect again. If he still hasn't received it, resend. If the prospect has received the material but hasn't reviewed it, reschedule your appointment. The prospect needs to have reviewed your material before you discuss it. This will limit the number of questions the prospect asks, since your material should have the basic facts about your program. It's ridiculous to tell the prospect things he can just as easily read for himself.)

You: Are you ready to join /name of program/ today?

(Always ask this question right up front. Remember, from time to time you're going to get an immediate yes.)

Prospect: Not yet, I need some questions answered.

You: Of course, I'm happy to help you, but I'd like to know if your questions are answered to your satisfaction if you'll be joining us today.

Note: Your job as a recruiter is NOT merely to provide information to a prospect. IT'S TO RECRUIT! This means you have to keep the discussion firmly centered on just one objective: recruiting your prospect. That's why this question is so important: if I provide the information you need, will you sign up? Real prospects will answer in the affirmative. Time-wasters will equivocate. Listen very hard to the answer so you know who you're dealing with.

Real Prospect: Yes, if you provide me with hard answers to my questions, I'm ready to sign up.

Or, Another Real Prospect: If you provide me with specific answers to my questions, I'm going to think over what you say and I'll be ready to talk to you again in a week.

Unreal Prospect: Well, now, not so fast. I don't like to be rushed. I need lots of extra time. I just can't make a commitment right now. I've got lumbago, the creek's rising, my kid's in jail and needs bail money, my mother-in-law's coming for a visit, *etc., etc., etc.*

The unreal prospect demands specific information (always hoping that your inability to supply it will provide him with just the excuse he needs to get rid of you) but is never willing to be tied down once you've provided it.

Your response to an unreal prospect: "Mr. Prospect, do you agree that we offer a superior opportunity?" Wait for his answer.

"Do you agree that you can make money from this opportunity?"

Wait for his answer.

"Now, Mr. Prospect, I want to work with you, but I need your assurance that if I put in the time and effort to provide you with all the information you need, to answer all your questions, you'll reciprocate by joining. I don't want to waste any of your time... and I don't want to waste any of my time. If you can assure me that if I get you what you want you'll join, let's go ahead and get started. But if you can't, let's just shake hands right here and end this thing."

Again, real prospects won't mind this kind of pointedness. They understand that you're running a business and must approach them in a businesslike fashion. They have legitimate questions and they want them treated seriously. But they know you are right to ask them to be serious, too. Approaching them in this open, honest, candid way will suit the real prospects just fine, thank you very much.

Unfortunately, the unreal prospect will not respond in this fashion. He'll make you feel as guilty as possible for addressing him in this perfectly reasonable straightforward way. He'll say things like, "You're so pushy." Or "I just can't be rushed." What he really is telling you is, "No matter how much information you give me, no matter how many good reasons you provide, I don't have the money to go ahead... the skills... the determination... the commitment... or the desire. But I cannot afford to tell you this, the blow would be too hard on my thin self-esteem, so I've got to turn this all around and make you feel you've blown this deal by handling me wrong, that I would have signed up if you'd known the magic way of dealing with me, but that because you didn't, you'll miss out on all the benefits of having me on your team."

Friend, this is the immemorial technique of the flatworm... to eschew responsibility and to thrust it, however unreasonably, on to someone else. And it's rampant in the opportunity field.

The sad fact is the majority of people you contact *won't* be real prospects. They *won't* have what it takes to succeed in this business... no matter how little you're asking of them. But they're *not* going to tell you this. No way! They're going to do everything possible to turn the blame to you... for saying the wrong thing, doing the wrong thing, thinking the wrong thing, representing the wrong company... for just getting out of bed that day and daring to talk to them!!!

In real life, when two people want to make a deal there can be lots of inelegant lumbering to the finish line. The presentation won't have to be perfect... the prospect won't have to be entirely organized and efficient. But, somehow, the matter will work out to both parties' satisfaction.

The way to ensure this result is to base your presentation on one simple sentence:

WHAT DOES IT TAKE FOR US TO DO BUSINESS TODAY?

Whenever you're in doubt in a presentation, use this line. When the prospect yaps on interminably and won't get to the point... when his objections get more and more trivial... when you just can't seem to get to an understanding, ask this question and then LISTEN.

If the prospect answers this question in a vague, unsatisfactory way, ASK IT AGAIN. Make it clear to the prospect that you want an agreement TODAY and that you're willing to do your part. WHAT YOU NEED TO KNOW IS WHAT THE PROSPECT WANTS.

Lots of people find it very, very difficult to be this straightforward with prospects. No wonder. Most people aren't very straightforward in their dealings with others, at any time. But when you're prospecting, lack of specificity is a costly snare. I've heard from my (usually new) independent distributors sufficiently often about how they've wasted an evening with a prospect only to find that the prospect really never had any intention of joining. This is criminal!!! This cannot happen if you keep asking, "But what does it take for us to do business NOW"... and listen carefully for the response.

Answering Objections, Moving Closer To The Close

Once you've secured agreement from the prospect that if his objections are satisfactorily answered, he'll join, then tackle the objections head on.

You: "I'd like to know, Mr. Prospect, just how many questions and objections we're talking about. And I'd like to confirm that when I've answered these to your satisfaction, you'll sign up. Is this correct?"

Now start attacking the questions/objections one by one, providing your best answers.

Note: again, I remind you that you may either not know an answer or may not have the best answer readily available. In this case, tell the prospect what you're going to do and when you'll provide the information. Then follow up accordingly.

Once you've answered each question/objection, ask the prospect if it has been handled to his *complete* satisfaction. If so, you're that much closer to a close. If not, find out what's missing. You must make sure you have given the prospect no reason not to close. You don't want to hear the irritating words, "I decided not to join because of your inadequate answer to one of my questions..."

Carry on through the prospect's questions/objections until they're finished. At this point, say: "Well, Mr. Prospect, I believe all your questions/objections have been handled to your satisfaction. Are you ready to complete the paperwork now for joining /name of your opportunity/?"

If the prospect is less than 100% committed, now's the moment when he'll probably try his last stalling technique — whatever he's told you before about his willingness to sign up once his objections have been answered. Sure, he made the agreement with you... but that was before he knew how thorough, persistent and dogged you were about doing — precisely what you said you were going to do!

Prospect: "Ur, well, you see it's like this... I'm not really ready to sign up yet..."

You: "Mr. Prospect, you and I have an agreement. I asked you if you'd sign up when your questions and objections were dealt with and on this basis we went ahead. I've done what I said I'd do... and it's only fair now to expect you to do what you said you'd do."

At this point, the prospect is cornered and people with even the least residue of the unreal prospect won't like this feeling at all. Why? Because they may have covered up the real reason for not going ahead — the primary reason being lack of money.

Prospect: "I'm convinced, but I just don't have any money."

Knowing what to do at this point divides the pro's from the greenhorns. Even pro's can take the occasional walk down the garden path with time-wasters and people who just won't own up to the facts of their personal situations. We live in a culture which constantly splashes up images of the good life, of what to do with your money. It constantly praises those with cash... and denigrates those without. In this situation, it's hard, very, very hard, for people without means to actually own up to their impoverished condition. And it's particularly hard for men to do so... since men so often define themselves exclusively in terms of the money they have. For a man to say, "I just can't do it because I don't have the money," cuts his masculinity to the core. Yes, it would be better if prospects in this sorry state would own up to the fact right away. But they don't.

Thus, your job in the closing process is to keep asking the prospect if you are moving to a close. The real prospect won't mind checking off progress to a close. Indeed, he'll admire your efficiency and organization. The unreal prospect, by comparison, will get more and more uneasy as the close approaches. For one thing, if you ask whether the close is closer, he'll have to lie more and more. And, unless this person is a complete liar, he'll provide you with signs of his nervousness and prevarication.

In any case, the minute you know the person is not a real prospect say, "Mr. Prospect, I'm very disappointed to find out that we haven't been moving to getting you off to a fast start in this opportunity. I've played fair with you... and I trusted that you were playing fair with me. Since you can't close today, what would you like to do now?"

Since the prospect is the problem, let the prospect suggest a way out of the difficulty. Wait and listen for his response.

Prospect: "Call me in a month and I'll see about joining."

Of course, the unreal prospect puts you off — again. He wants to be a player but cannot really play. So he plays in his own way... by forcing you to dance to his tune. Outrageous! Thus, before agreeing to this proposition, try the seriousness test again.

You: "I'll be happy to call you in a month, Mr. Prospect, if you realistically think that at that time you'll be ready to join. What makes you think that in 30 days you'll be any more ready to join than now?"

Wait and listen for his answer. The person who's sincerely trying to work with you and who really wants to join the opportunity, may well have a problem now... but he will have thought over what's likely to be different at the time he suggests for action. Real prospects always have specific answers. Unreal prospects will continue to be vague. Their answer will be something like this, "Well, I just think things will be better, that's all." That's not an answer, dear friend, it's an anti-answer. It doesn't move you closer to a close... it just prolongs the flatworm's game.

If you think what you've heard is positive, schedule an appointment for 30 days hence. If you don't think it's positive, say, "Mr. Prospect, with all due respect, what you're saying just isn't convincing. What I'd like to do is leave you with my telephone number. As you yourself have admitted, I represent a superior opportunity and one in which you yourself told me you think you could profit. When you're ready to take advantage of this opportunity, call me. You'll find me more than ready to be of assistance to you." Then end the call pleasantly and go on to the next prospect.

Note: some day when you've got nothing better to do, get on the phone and call a few of these "prospects" and seek to re-qualify them. Things really do change in people's lives. Why, in just the last couple of weeks two prospects that I used this technique with have actually called to join my MLM organizations. But if they hadn't, each would have still received a call from me somewhere down the line, pointedly asking them if they were — at last! — ready to join my organizations and start raking in the benefits they already knew about!

At Closing

As soon as you have polished off all the prospect's objections, it's time to sign the prospect up as your newest independent distributor. Confirm that the prospect has the paperwork you've sent. Now ask the prospect to fill it out while you're on the phone. Go through the application point by point right to the end. Then ask him to send the original (plus applicable payment) to the company, keep a copy for himself, and send you a copy, too, for your files. You can then move on to what he needs to do next to get off to a fast start.

By following these techniques, you'll get two benefits and you'll get them faster, namely 1) shaking off unreal prospects sooner so they waste less and less of your time, and 2) signing up real prospects faster so you can get them started on a profitable career in your opportunity sooner. Congratulations!

Last Words On Follow-Up

Despite our advanced state of telecommunications, it can still be very difficult to get in touch with people. It's therefore helpful to have guidelines about how often you should attempt to do so.

- When a person sends you an indication he wants more information on your opportunity, make three follow-up phone calls to attempt to connect. Each time leave a full message, thus:

"My name is /name/. You responded to an ad for details on /name of opportunity/. I'd like to discuss this with you. Please call me at /number/ to do so."

The second message should be the same except you should say it's your second message.

The third message should say, "My name is /name/. This is my third phone call to follow up your response to our ad for /name of opportunity./ Unfortunately this is my last phone call so if you'd like details about how to profit from this company, you must call me."

If you like and have the time, follow this third phone call up with a template letter laying out the most compelling reasons for joining the company and enclosing an application. If you're using a self-mailer that can be sent for the price of a first-class stamp, send that instead. But don't hold your breath. A person who can ignore three phone calls after asking for information can easily ignore this marketing communication, too.

- If a person isn't available when you call for a scheduled appointment, leave this message on his answering machine,

"This is /name./ I'm calling for our scheduled appointment to discuss your joining /name of opportunity./ I'm sorry you weren't able to keep this appointment and wish you had let me know. Please call me at /number/ to reschedule."

If this person doesn't call back, my personal inclination is to drop him off my Christmas card list and cease further communications. However, *you* talked to him. If you think there's hope based on what you've heard, call back in a couple of weeks to requalify the prospect and, if what you hear is positive, reschedule an appointment.

What I'm trying to stress in this chapter is simply this: it's your job to develop a client-closing *system*. Part of this system is constantly checking with your prospect to ensure that, yes, he is a prospect… that he's moving closer to a close… and that the chances of his joining your team are constantly improving. You are under no obligation to work with anyone who won't work with you… who won't meet your demand for reasonable professional behavior. Remember,

- you are not in the business of sending out "literature";
- you are not in the business of answering objections for people who don't have the means of joining your team;
- you are not in the business of catering to the slothful, the procrastinating, the impoverished, the disorganized, the stupid, the torpid, the deceitful, the inefficient, or the cheerful liars who think nothing of leading you on, and are astonished that you are bothered by their destructive habits.

Your job, dear friend, is a simple one: to perfect your case, to know all objections to it and to answer them forthrightly, and to ensure that you are always working with a prospect who is honestly working with you to get the information he needs so he can become a useful member of your team.

It is therefore your responsibility to keep probing to ensure that your prospect is really a prospect… and to move the closing process briskly along, to either get rid of the flatworm as soon as possible or achieve the result you really wanted all along: recruit another qualified independent distributor as soon as possible and so spur the growth of your organization. I feel confident this chapter will help you achieve both goals more efficiently.

CHAPTER 5

M
L
M

GETTING YOUR NEW DISTRIBUTOR OFF TO THE BEST POSSIBLE START

"A bird in the hand" the old saw goes, "is worth more than two in the bush." The same, dear reader, is true of distributors. Once you've got 'em, your job is to hold 'em. Predictably, I've got something to say about the most sensible ways of doing that.

The key to getting a distributor off to a good start is:

- getting him/her to make a commitment to working the program;

- developing a sensible plan that fits into the distributor's life, asks him to make the fewest changes and recognizes his realistic level of commitment;

- providing adequate technical assistance with marketing communications, leads, telemarketing and other support, and

- getting the distributor success at the earliest possible moment, thereby confirming the wisdom of his/her decision and spurring his/her enthusiasm and commitment.

Let's look at each of these points.

Getting The Necessary Distributor Commitment

Lots of distributors suffer from the completely ridiculous delusion that network marketing is some kind of "get rich quick" scheme; that all they have to do is sign up, lick a couple of stamps, and lay back awaiting mail-order millions. Anyone who has ever run a successful business, of course, always finds it hard to understand where such adolescent fantasies originate and why they are seemingly impossible to eradicate. Nonetheless, the fantasies endure.

Let's be clear about something. You can make money in network marketing, often times *lots and lots* of money. But it's not effortless. It does take time. It does take a plan. It does take the suitable deployment of scarce resources. It does take intelligence. It does take constant consideration and discernment. It does take persistence. It does take a thick skin. It does take the ability to perfect sales closing skills. It does take regular effort.

It does, in short, take your active commitment not only to your own success but achieving that success along with and because of others in your organization achieving success, too.

The importance of this "active commitment" cannot be overstated. And, like all resources and benefits, it's in very short supply among opportunity seekers. Many of these people are like wildebeest on the African veldt... roaming from waterhole to waterhole, lingering just long enough to get a taste... never stopping long enough to build, only to experience. This is, of course, the exact antithesis of what it takes to build a business.

If you are going to succeed in network marketing you are going to have to commit yourself not only to achieving success with and through others but achieving this success with and through a particular company. This means research.

Personally, I never believe in making a commitment lightly. To me commitment is the essential basis of success and before I make such a commitment I want to be absolutely sure I am making the right decision. As we've already discussed, this means:

- reviewing many opportunities;

- seeing which ones are the most solid, substantial, productive and long-lasting;

- scrutinizing and re-scrutinizing to be absolutely sure you're not making the wrong decision, and only then

- deciding on the opportunity and committing yourself to it.

Unfortunately, undertaking this kind of thoughtful review process is precisely what most people do not do. They ask for a bunch of information packages, make only the most cursory examination (if any examination at all) and carelessly select a company. Once all their sales materials arrive, they do a little rushing about, seeing if anyone is going to be interested in what they've got. Predictably, most people aren't very interested and as this lack of interest grows, the distributor's limited interest wanes... until he resumes the all-too-familiar search process, requesting more information packages, making more cursory examinations, *etc*.

Does this sound familiar? It ought to... it's how the vast majority of independent distributors approach the whole business of selecting their golden opportunity!

Keep in mind, however, that active commitment can only come after you have thoroughly reviewed and analyzed

- who and where you are

- what you want

- the skills you have

- what you must do, and
- what the company will do to help you achieve success.

Commitment is never born in a vacuum; it can only come after careful scrutiny and consideration.

In this connection, review who and where you are:

- Do you have adequate time for the opportunity you are considering?
- Do you have adequate resources?
- Do you have adequate strength and health?
- Are you over committed on other fronts so that any involvement in this opportunity is doomed to failure?

While I was writing this chapter I chanced to see an info-mercial on starting a home-business. Because the manipulators who put on this program wanted the maximum number of people to attend their home-office expo, they made it seem like opening and running a successful home-based business was like a walk in the park. They said things like "anyone can have a successful home-based business," and downplayed the need for technical skills. Why, they actually said that people didn't even need computers and fax machines to succeed! It's the old "anyone can do it" mantra with a vengeance.

But this is wrong, wrong, wrong. Not everyone can succeed either in a home-based business or in a network marketing opportunity (most of which are home-based, after all). There are preconditions for success and if you don't have them, you're going to find it very difficult if not impossible to succeed. Just "wanting a few more bucks every month" isn't nearly enough.

Review What You Want

We have now entered the era when more and more people want to be entertained, want leisure, want pampering, want to "get away from it all." Under the circumstances it's hardly surprising that the sports-entertainment business has zoomed up as one of America's premier growth industries. As "real life" gets more tiresome and demanding and as the population ages, this trend is likely only to grow stronger. The real question is, "Where's the money coming from to pay for all this leisure time?" Ah, there's the rub!

You don't have a lot of people going around saying, "If you want the good life and weren't born with a trust fund, you're going to have to sacrifice to get it." Sacrifice is a concept lots of Americans feel very uncomfortable with. The fact that other generations of Americans have regularly deferred gratification, have regularly made decisions which defer present gratification for future wealth, now seems irrelevant to many. The Now Generation wants instant leisure, instant wealth, instant success.

GET REAL!!!

If you're going to make money in network marketing, you're going to have to sacrifice. I know.

For many years, I assiduously avoided network marketing. I didn't like the kind of witless people that seemed to proliferate in its ranks. I didn't like the kinds of glossy, vulgar, ill-bred, shiftless, irresponsible people who were it's principal spokespeople. I didn't like the reckless claims, distortions and outright lies of its marketing communications. And I thought that its product lines were often laughable... not merely for their lack of quality but also for their ludicrously inflated prices.

All in all, I thought, network marketing was a joke. But because many of the people who buy my books and reports and run cards in my card-deck are in network marketing, I was in a position to review developments without having to make a commitment.

Over time it became apparent to me that the network marketing concept per se was sound... the basic idea of recruiting a productive distributor who recruits a productive distributor, and so on through an infinite number of levels. What was basically wrong, however, was that the network marketing companies themselves failed to provide the necessary technical assistance to ensure that their distributors (who were, after all, largely people without any business experience) could succeed; that they could profit from the concept of network marketing through the apt use of thorough company-generated technical assistance.

Without exception, the network marketing industry ignored the legitimate and pressing needs of their independent distributors... either because they didn't care about these needs... or because, once they'd discerned the needs, they hadn't a clue about how to provide for them. Either way, it was an industry-wide plague of unparalleled stupidity.

This basic flaw engendered all the problems which I saw every day in the industry. Instead of providing step-by-step assistance to independent distributors, the morons who run most network marketing companies focused instead on:

■ bragging about their products. "Our products are so good," they said (and say), "they'll sell themselves."

■ making money by selling overpriced "distributor packages." "Since we can't make money *through* distributor sales," they reckoned (and reckon), "we'll make money by selling *to* distributors."

■ creeping into the printing business. This ensured (and still ensures) a steady profit stream, since they encourage the belief that one more brochure, one more flyer, one more four-color publication will surely get someone to sign up.

■ either "warm marketing" and/or "direct mail" marketing. They benefited (and still benefit) from "warm marketing" because they know that people will support their friends and family to a significant extent... even if they have no use for the product being purchased. Thus, the companies know they can succeed simply by exploiting the good will and supportiveness inherent in virtually all Americans. They also know that because most people hate personal and telephone contact and anything remotely connected to "sales", that they'd invest heavily (as they still do) in costly direct-mail marketing... even though any of them with a shred of responsibility know that this is a money-losing proposition for the vast majority of those using it.

Lack of substantive technical assistance to independent distributors bred all the maggots in the industry and it was the maggots, and their manifestations, that responsible people like me so rightly detested (and continue to detest today).

The cure to all this was not, as the maggots believed, more hype, more lies, more deception, more supposedly gigantic pay-checks (without details on how to achieve them). No, indeed: the cure is step-by-step technical assistance of the kind embodied in The L.A.N.T. SYSTEM™, a system that doesn't rely on inflated claims but on the realization that building a business takes a solid company, believable benefits, an achievable plan, and step-by-step distributor guidelines, constantly reviewed and improved.

While I got into network marketing knowing of its defects, it was only with an incomplete idea that I would personally be shortly rectifying them! This meant sacrifice... it meant:

- reviewing what limited technical support systems existed;

- analyzing the needs of independent distributors;

- improving marketing communications so they were more benefit-rich and client-centered;

- researching, adopting, creating and perfecting a variety of lead-generating mechanisms;

- integrating telemarketing support into the system and experimenting with both personnel and means to deliver effective telemarketing support.

All this took time, money and lots of mental dedication.

There were lots of vested interests, you see, who didn't want this system to succeed and who were perfectly content with the extraordinarily imperfect status quo. The mere fact that this status quo failed to work for millions of independent distributors was of no concern to these people — certain presidents of network marketing companies, their directors of marketing, the people who did their printing, the companies that sold advertising and rented mailing lists, *etc.*, *etc.*, *etc.* All systems, of course, have their vested interests, but the network marketing industry has its in spades. Moreover, because of the lack of independent distributor cohesion, it's easy to let the interests of such people slide when one's own interests are so much more compelling.

Because of such people, you've got to be extra careful as you both review opportunities and work them. You must resolve what I resolved, namely to:

- scrutinize the company carefully. Understand how money is made in this company and whether you can make money with and through it.

- set a challenging but achievable financial goal;

- set quarterly, monthly, and weekly recruiting and sales objectives;

- review the company marketing communications to see if they adequately communicate the benefits of belonging to and working this opportunity;

- create your own marketing communications to communicate benefits if you find (as you usually will) the company materials lacking;

- explore all available prospect lead generating options, taking the time to understand how they work and considering how to make them available not just to yourself, but to the people you recruit into your organization;

- assess all your prospects. All prospects, as you know now, are not equal. You need to take the time to quiz prospects, to see which of them are more valuable, worth investing in;

- make sure the people you recruit have both the time and other resources to invest in making the opportunity a success and that they'll do what's necessary to make their experience (and your involvement) profitable.

- take the time you need to review what you (and the members of your organization) do, what works, what doesn't, and to make any changes.

Sadly, if you're in the usual, pedestrian MLM company, you're not going to get much, if any, assistance doing these things. Instead you'll find, as I have, that company officials do little or nothing to help you. I have never understood this stupid and self-defeating behavior, but it is absolutely characteristic of the vast majority of network marketing owners and employees. To them, the independent distributor is a nuisance, to be tolerated at best, and all too often ignored and dismissed.

Thus, if you're going to succeed in network marketing you need to understand that the primary responsibility for your success is going to fall upon — you! You're going to need to set the objectives, develop the marketing communications, and general your growing army.

To be sure, if you don't wish to assume either this responsibility or this leadership role, you do have other options (besides dropping out altogether). You can search for those relatively rare companies which are eager to assist you and which have established useful means for doing so, or you can work with recognized leaders who have developed productive success systems. This book assists you with both alternatives.

But if you will not take these alternatives, then you are left with only two options: either 1) become a leader and do what's necessary for you and your organization to succeed, or 2) proceed haltingly and unintelligently, the way the vast majority of people in network marketing do — with entirely predictable and entirely avoidable results.

∎ The Skills You Have

Unlike the people I saw on the telly pushing their home-business expo, I don't believe that anyone, no matter how poor their skill level, can succeed either in a home-based or network marketing opportunity. Life may be unfair, but the chance for rewards is higher when you are more highly skilled.

In this connection, to succeed in network marketing you need:

- **good organizational skills.** If this isn't apparent by now, you've missed a major point in this guide.

- **computer skills.** Yes, you can probably make a go of it without being computer literate, but why bother? My computer is an essential factor in my ability to connect with and motivate so many people. I couldn't possibly have risen in three network marketing companies so quickly if I hadn't mastered this machine.

- **good communications skills.** If you join a network marketing opportunity where the company doesn't feel that its job is to provide you with client-centered marketing communications and you either can't or won't use trained copywriters like those at my National Copywriting Center, you had better learn how to write benefit-rich prose yourself. Otherwise, pack it in now because if you can't do it, you're going to lose out. After all, you're competing against masters like me.

- **good telephone skills.** The same applies to the phone. You're not going to be able to build a profitable network marketing distributor force without mastering the phone.

- **change skills.** As technology advantages, what made sense to do today, won't make sense tomorrow. The ability to change is as much a skill as the ability to create and generate a client-centered brochure (or computer diskette!)

∎ What You Must Do

There's no point making a commitment if you don't know what you must do to succeed and don't know if you can do it. Success in network marketing is predicated upon:

- beneficial products, constantly improved and expanded;
- client-centered marketing communications that clearly bring the benefits of these products to designated publics;
- marketing communications that clearly instruct independent distributors on how to both sell products and recruit other independent distributors;
- the apt use of many lead-generating vehicles, and
- the apt use of lead-qualifying and lead-closing telemarketing.

In an ideal universe, your network marketing company would focus on providing assistance in all these areas. But you already know better. If you're in a network marketing company now, you already know how little of this your company does; how much of it they leave for you to do.

If you're going to achieve success in network marketing, either

- the company must provide you with this kind of thorough technical assistance, or
- you must provide yourself with it, or
- you must engage the services of The L.A.N.T. SYSTEM™.

It's up to you. If you don't do any of these three things, you're going to fail. It's as simple as that. So, resolve here and now that you'll either:

- get the company to revolutionize its approach to marketing either internally or by engaging The L.A.N.T. SYSTEM™, or
- do the revolutionizing yourself, or
- make it easy on yourself by engaging The L.A.N.T. SYSTEM™ yourself.

There's no point being committed if you're not going to do what's necessary to succeed. Commitment without a technical basis for success is just plain masochism.

▮ What The Company Must Do

Over time, I've asked hundreds of distributors if they feel their company adequately sustains them from a marketing standpoint. The smart ones know the companies are remiss. They join because they like the lure of easy money, because they like the product lines, because they feel they can overcome the companies' manifest marketing deficiencies through their own efforts and expertise. This isn't good enough.

Now that The L.A.N.T. SYSTEM™ exists, you can go to the CEO of your company and tell him/her about this System and advocate that your network marketing company start using it. If this CEO understands his business (a big "if"), he'll understand that his company cannot grow without supporting the independent distributor. He'll also be willing to acknowledge (something very painful but necessary in the growth process) that he hasn't done as much as he could to sustain this crucial person and that the time has come to review alternatives. When he understands that The L.A.N.T. SYSTEM™ will not only support independent distributors like you but actually make the company money right away, he ought to jump for joy.

If he doesn't, ask why. The low-grade MLM CEO will say something stupid like one CEO told me during the writing of this resource: "I give my independent distributors a company brochure and tell them to figure the rest out for themselves." And this man claims to be a forward-looking company president!!! In fact, he's a pompous, narrow-minded, probably irredeemable fool.

Friend, I beg you: don't even think about being committed to a company unless that company is as committed to your own success as it is to its own. Indeed, unless it recognizes that its success is inextricably linked to yours. Commitment without reference to the corporate culture and marketing plan of the company you've selected is a fool's commitment, one destined to wane and embitter. Proceed accordingly!

While you yourself may not have gone through this commitment process personally, now that you know how important it is, I trust you will share the need for this kind of commitment with your distributors. It's important that they're willing to give this opportunity time and effort. In this connection, I think, for instance, of an individual who, in my early days in network marketing, signed up one week... and resigned the next, having done absolutely nothing.

Now this can't happen in my organization. Why? Because I demand of people particularly on my first line that they make at least a six-month commitment, not just to being a member but to making an active commitment on behalf of the program. I don't want people to sign up merely to sit around and do nothing. I want them to understand that there is work to do to achieve success. I want them to know that I work... and I want them to know that I expect them to work, too. If a person won't do this, if he won't agree to follow the steps that I have now proven lead one to success in network marketing, I suggest they go elsewhere. It's better to let them go now, since it's certain that if they come into the program with such a bad attitude and without a pledge to conform to a winning system, that there will be more trouble and disappointment down the road.

Having once secured their commitment that they'll work... I then work with them to create a sensible plan, a plan that will result in the fastest and greatest success possible given the amount of work and resources they're prepared to invest.

▮ Developing A Sensible Plan

Commitment, while essential, is never enough to ensure success. Success is the result of a realistic plan regularly worked. Your master independent distributor plan should include:

- weekly time commitment
- monthly investment quota
- monthly recruitment objective
- downline technical assistance goal.

Here's what a typical plan might look like for the average distributor in my Staff of Life/Ad-Net organizations:

■ Weekly Time Commitment

5 hours. This time is to be used for arranging to get leads, qualifying leads, sending marketing communications, following up with closing calls, continuing education about the program, working with downline members.

■ Monthly Investment Quota

$300. This sum pays for monthly Ad-Net fees and for product purchase at the $90 level for The Staff of LIfe, self-mailers, additional lead requirements beyond prospect leads supplied by Ad-Net, postage, telephone, fax, *etc.*

■ Monthly Recruitment Objective

No one should ever be in MLM without having a monthly recruiting objective. While this number will vary depending on many factors, the lowest acceptable number is one new person on the distributor's first level per month. All activities should be regulated to achieving this minimum number. Remember, to achieve the objective of "The Awesome Power of One" System, each of your distributors must also recruit at least one person per month!

■ Downline Technical Assistance

In network marketing, one never works entirely for oneself. One is always part of a team, a team which must and should be constantly expanding. Thus, part of your time must be spent not just recruiting but working with existing downline members. They must understand the system and work to replicate it. You must make time to call them, assess their performance, identify weak-spots and overcome them. Providing downline technical assistance must be a part of every successful marketing plan. The fact that so many people fail in MLM is as clear proof as necessary that this central idea has not made it into the operations of the vast majority of independent distributors.

Key Aspects Of Your Plan

For a plan to work, it must be:

- clear on its objective
- short
- specific

- fit in with your life
- provide adequate technical assistance
- recorded
- reviewed
- changed as necessary.

▮ Clear On Objective

What's the point of a plan without a destination? Your plan needs to set forth your income objectives by date and just how many active independent distributors you'll need to accomplish this objective. Don't just say, "I want to make as much money as possible." Say, "to make my /precise income objective/ by /date/ I need to recruit /so many people on your first line/, /so many people on your second line/", *etc*. Personally, I ardently believe in management by objectives to organize key aspects of my life, including the development of my network marketing empire. Join me! Decide on a reasonable but challenging objective. Then look at a calendar and decide just when you want it.

▮ Short

In my experience, long, complicated plans are doomed plans. So, keep yours short and sweet. A single page should be more than adequate. You want something, after all, that covers the subject but which you can easily post where you can see it every day.

▮ Specific

Your plan is no place for vagueness. Be precise about:

- what your objective is (such as, two new people on your first line every month)
- how much time you intend to dedicate to achieving this objective
- how much money you have to invest
- how you intend to get client-centered marketing communications
- where your leads are coming from and how many you'll need
- how many telephone calls for both qualifying prospects leads and closing them you intend to make every week.

Right now if you asked the overwhelming majority of people in network marketing just what they were working for, they'd say something vague like "financial independence." And if you asked them precisely how they intended to achieve this... and precisely when, they couldn't tell you. Indeed, they'd probably stand there looking vacant, ridiculously perplexed.

Dear friend, this can't be you. YOU'VE got to know precisely where you're going. Knowing where you're going assists in the following crucial ways:

- You stay focused. Once you've determined your destination, you'll know whether any given activity either helps or hinders you from reaching it. You'll have a much clearer sense of what you should do — and what you should avoid doing. You can determine what's important... and what is unimportant, no matter what it may appear to be.

- You enlist the support of your subconscious mind. If you constantly keep before you just what you want to achieve, you'll find that your subconscious mind will work, yes, even while you're sleeping, to help you cull through ideas and determine the best ones that make sense for your situation. If the mind doesn't have a destination to focus on, it will not be of the utmost assistance to you.

- You have a much greater likelihood of reaching your goal. If you don't know where you're going, you can't get there. Over the course of many years, during which I've become more and more goal-oriented, I'm constantly amazed that the shear act of setting a goal and setting the strategy for reaching it puts me, almost immediately, within measurable distance of achieving that goal. Whatever distance remains can be dealt with by perfecting any given plan and perfecting the means used to achieve it.

What's astonishing to me is how few people make these kinds of plans. I, however, am one of them. Indeed, you might say I'm a plan fanatic. I don't just map my plan for the day or a week... but for a year at least. Indeed, for certain large objectives I have a five-year plan. So should you. If achieving success in network marketing is really important to you, you can't afford not to.

▐ Your Plan Must Fit Into Your Life

As every dietitian knows, if you ask a client to make too many lifestyle changes all at once, it's just not going to happen. Thus, one key to successful planning is to start with a plan that asks you to make fewest changes in your life. If, for instance, you find yourself coming home from your office exhausted at 7 p.m. most nights, it's unrealistic to think you could make two hours of evening telephone calls. 30 minutes is more likely. Thus:

- be clear about what you have to do;

- then examine your own life to see if you can actually achieve so much

    ▐ do an analysis of an average week of your life to determine how much free time you really have;

    ▐ look at how you feel during the time you have available. Are you really alert enough to use this time for recruitment?

■ do you have the available financial and other resources you think you have? It's no good saying you can invest $75 a week, when all you have is $30 and that any greater transfer of funds at this moment would cause other problems.

■ can you really rearrange your activities to provide for the things you need to accomplish in developing your business?

After having worked with literally thousands of people starting and developing businesses, I am clear about one thing: a clear grasp of reality is essential at all times. If you're the kind of person who's been working banker's hours for 13 years, who likes to break every 45 minutes for a chat at the water cooler, who doesn't like to make decisions and doesn't have a lot of experience doing so, who hasn't been responsible for determining how money's to be spent and for making the difficult decisions about priorities, thinking that you're going to change all this quickly to become a highly focused, highly goal-oriented, highly responsible, self-motivated network marketer probably just isn't in the cards. Instead, see yourself precisely as you are and proceed accordingly.

Newcomers to network marketing generally make two very serious mistakes: they don't know anything about how network marketing works as a money-making entity and they don't understand what's truly possible given their own personalities, behavior and work patterns.

I have a friend, for instance, who's been intrigued for years about my business and regularly tells me that he'd like to be able to "cash in" the way I've done. Yet, consider how he approaches becoming a tycoon:

- he's computer illiterate

- adamant he won't work after 5 p.m.

- would never conceive of working on a week-end or holiday

- doesn't have an answering machine, and, I think,

- would probably faint if he had to ask for an order.

Unsurprisingly, I have never pressed the matter about assisting him in business and probably never will. The last straw was when I gave him a copy of one of my business-development books as a present when I stayed a week-end. When I came back a year later the book had never been opened.

No, this man is not a candidate for network marketing or any other business benefits.

Just be sure you are.

▮ Provides Adequate Technical Assistance

As you probably already know, ordinarily the last time you hear from your upline "support" is the day you sign up into his organization. This, of course, is outrageous, a major reason why both upline and downline members fail in MLM. Just in case you haven't already received this message, let me stress it again: if you go into network marketing without having a clear understanding that providing ongoing technical assistance to the people you recruit is essential you are ensuring your failure — and theirs. Shame on you!

By "adequate" technical assistance, I mean:

- working with the downline supporter to ensure he/she understands the benefits of the company so that he/she can sell it to any recruit;

- knowing the objections to joining... and the best responses to them;

- vowing to maintain regular, ongoing contact with independent distributors;

- making oneself available to assist in closing prospects the independent distributor is working with;

- asking for regular reports from downline members to oversee progress.

To achieve your goal in network marketing, you must continue your own recruiting... and you must assist others in your organization to recruit. It is never enough just to build your own first line. You must, instead, provide ongoing technical assistance to ensure that others build their lines, too.

Does this mean providing technical assistance to everyone? Let me be very clear in my answer to this question.

YOU ARE OBLIGED TO PROVIDE TECHNICAL ASSISTANCE ONLY TO THOSE PEOPLE WHO ARE WILLING TO COMMIT THEMSELVES AND TO WORK TO IMPLEMENT THEIR PLAN.

With the best will in the world, you'll find yourself with drones in your organization. Because the belief is so prevalent in network marketing that you have to do nothing to succeed, even though your scrutiny is thorough, some plausible liar will creep through to bedevil you. Plan for it.

If this happens,

- call this back-sliding distributor on every infraction. Is his periodic situation report late, or does he fail to make any report at all? Call him on it! Does he fail to familiarize himself with the program? Doesn't bother to get leads, or having got leads fail to qualify them? Call him on it!

- ask the independent distributor to work with you... and let him know what's going to happen if he doesn't.

- If his back-sliding continues, give him a warning. Say, "I want to work with you, but if you cannot or will not participate as an active member of my team, you will force me to spend my limited resources elsewhere. Will you work as a member of my team, setting objectives, and working to achieve them?"

- If the answer is vague, say, "Unfortunately, I find your answer unsatisfactory." Then give him some tasks to perform and let him know that if they're not done in apple-pie order, you're going to suspend your assistance indefinitely.

- If the person still fails to cooperate, just send him a note indicating that when he's ready to perform as a working member of your team, you'll be glad to hear from him. Then just ignore him.

Dear reader: it would be nice if all the world were as conscientious as you and me; if people reasonably assessed their situations and resources and pledged to do just what they could reasonably accomplish in a given period. But people aren't this way. They constantly overpledge and underperform. And there's not a great deal you can do about it. I've been carrying on an informal survey for years now noting the hundreds of ways, both mundane and ingenious, people use to defeat themselves and ensure their lack of success.

I think for instant of a young independent distributor who came to me some months ago wanting a job. Since he was bright and a graduate of Harvard, I had no hesitation in giving him one. Then over the next months, I watched him do everything to destroy the good opinion I had of him.

- He was perpetually late in arriving;

- was never prepared;

- failed to deal with customers in anywhere near a satisfactory manner;

- constantly complained about his duties, *etc., etc., etc.*

Yet throughout the blighted period when I employed him, he constantly asked for more and more responsibility, continually telling me how much better he'd do if only he had more to do.

In short order I came to despise this creature and of course after just a few short months of "service" I fired him. His reaction? Apoplectic! He wrote me letter after letter setting forth all my sins, caricaturing me as a monster of unbelievable sins and improbable iniquities. My *real* sin? Giving him a chance. Asking him to behave like an adult and provide a fair service for a fair fee. Reviewing his conduct and asking him to improve. Being insistent that poor service could not be rewarded for all that he was an honor's graduate of The World's Greatest University. In his last letter to me, received while I was writing this book, this poor, contemptible creature described himself as a "near vagrant" and told me how much he needed money. I laughed aloud...

... people who exhibit self-defeating behaviors always expect others to understand, to empathize, to assist them, to overlook the messes they're so expert in creating, and to keep providing for them. They seem incapable of understanding that focused, goal-oriented people like you and me cannot afford to squander our deep humanitarian impulses on people like this, people who will not follow simple directions, will not work hard to achieve results yet who expect us to continue to cater to them.

Such contemptibles flourish in the network marketing industry (indeed, the fellow cited above was a man who failed as an independent distributor through his poor habits... and then turned around and blamed the product, the company, the industry... everything but his own load of inadequacies). Your job is to give them a chance, to supply them with the opening assistance you supply to everyone, to monitor their results carefully, to discipline early, and to jettison as soon as you get a whiff of their characteristic incompetence and unwillingness to reform. We are not, dear friend, in the business of reforming the world. We are in the business of prospering through network marketing. And we must not allow the many who would sap our strength and derail our enterprise to have the slightest opportunity for doing so. Or you will find yourself like the miserable example of my Harvard graduate whom I saw while writing this chapter wandering in Harvard Square in dirty, torn clothes, a pony tail, looking for all the world (and smelling too in my experience) like the tramp he seemed determined to become and which he was determined to blame me for attempting to help him avoid.

■ Your Plan Must Be Recorded

Your plan can't just be in your head. Ask the overwhelming majority of people in network marketing if they have a plan. Most will say no. Ask them if they have a written plan, and they'll virtually all say no. Is there any wonder most will also fail?

I recommend keeping your plan in two places: in computer and on hard copy posted where you can see it every day.

If your plan is on computer, call it up daily to see if you are reaching your targets. If it's posted, keep it prominent so you can look at it and see if you're making progress towards your goals.

Make sure that you've signed and dated this plan. You need to look at it as a contract you've signed with yourself, as binding as any other contract in your life and arguably more important.

The great planless majority may scoff at you because you're so organized, so determined. Let them. You'll not only laugh last, you'll do so in some comfortable spot.

▮ Review Your Plan

Particularly the first time you create a plan, it's likely to suffer from any number of imperfections. Perhaps you've underestimated what you're capable of, how long it will take to build your empire and what you've got to do. More likely, you've overestimated the results just a tad. Well, there's no sin in either... so long as you adjust the plan. Your goal, remember, is a plan that's at once reachable and challenging.

How often should you review your plan? At least monthly. Take the last Sunday of any given month to review your plan and make adjustments. Find out what's working... and why. Find out what's not working and what you can do about it.

The more you plan, the more you review, the better your planning process will become until you can write a meaningful plan for six months off the top of your head, feeling confident because of your seasoned experience that you can meet your objectives comfortably yet briskly.

▮ Change As Necessary

As your life changes, for good and ill, your plan must change. It's ridiculous to abide by a plan that just doesn't make sense given your altered circumstances. When, for instance, I determined to pay off my home mortgage in just two years (instead of continuing to make monthly payments over the course of 20 years), I had to change the way I made money so that I could make more. Ergo, my plan had to change, too.

When changing your plan be clear about what you want. Brainstorm all the means of achieving it. Then select the means that make the most sense given your current situation and having reviewed all your resources, from money in the bank to energy in the body. Conceive a new plan accordingly.

▮ Congratulate Yourself As You Achieve Your Objectives

One more thing. Give yourself some meaningful "attaboys." I don't just mean the occasional chocolate bar, either; I'm talking about something really good. Although I have been a goal-oriented person since I was a kid, I have not been a self-commending one until fairly recently in my development. I set goals, I sacrificed to reach them, I reached them... then I set other goals, *etc.* This left out one very important part of the cycle: CONGRATULATING YOURSELF.

In a world as self-absorbed as ours is, you cannot expect anyone to appreciate the goals you set for yourself and to understand just what you have to go through to reach them. Accept this. Thus, if you want to be congratulated for all you've done, congratulate yourself.

When you've set yourself a meaningful network marketing goal, determine at the same moment just what you'll give yourself when you get there. Do you like to travel? Is acquiring fine art your secret indulgence? What about a Jacuzzi or spa from whence you can field calls to your independent distributors, pampering yourself, yet still making money? It's your decision. Everything you desire should be considered. Nothing should be left out. You see, this is YOUR dream... and no one else's. It must be something *you* want, something which will assist in motivating *your* success.

In other books, I have written about the need to post a picture or visual representation of the desired item, to put it where you can see it every day. I still adhere to this belief. The more you think about what you want... the more likely you are to do what's necessary to achieve it.

The important thing is that what you select be worthy of you and the work and sacrifices you must make to achieve it. Don't select some picayune item of no importance. That can hardly be motivational!

When you've achieved your objective, don't wait to reward yourself. You've earned it. There's no time like the present for enjoying it. Let me know what you've selected, for you see, I love to hear from the successful and enjoy knowing what help I've been in helping them achieve one more thing their hearts desire!

CHAPTER 6

KEEPING YOUR INDEPENDENT DISTRIBUTORS ON THEIR TOES AND YOUR ORGANIZATION GROWING

You've worked hard — very hard — to recruit your distributors. Now you've got to work equally hard to keep them — so they can keep producing for you.

One of the amazing things to me about the network marketing literature is how little space and consideration is given to the matter of maintaining productive independent contractors. That's a big mistake. What's the point of going through all the effort of recruitment if you don't reap a continuing benefit? Perhaps commentators don't bother with this subject because they think that keeping distributors is a piece of cake; that all you have to do is get them in and move on to the next recruiting scenario. But if this is what they think, they're ridiculously wrong. Keeping distributors in your organization and keeping them productive is most assuredly *not* a piece of cake. And just like recruiting, maintaining distributors demands a strategy. Here it is:

- make keeping distributors a priority

- make sure each distributor has a realistic plan

- talk to them at regular intervals

- make leads available

- develop a group newsletter

- prod the company to publicize group successes.

▌ Make Keeping Distributors A Priority

Independent distributors are irritatingly casual about the people they recruit. If you talk to most distributors, although they may recognize that their success in network marketing is the result of their distributors producing, they make absolutely no effort to assist this process. They seem to think that their job is over once the distributor has signed on the dotted line. Friend, if this is you, GET REAL. That's precisely when your job *BEGINS*. Which is why you've got to make keeping your distributors a priority.

Once you've recruited a distributor it's up to you to enter into a bargain with your recruit. Let this person know that your relationship will grow from this point, not diminish. Let this person know that you understand that your success is bound up in his/hers. Let this person know how you work...

- just what kind of distributor support you provide;
- how often;
- what's reasonable for the distributor to expect from you;
- what he should do to help himself.

Make it clear to the distributor that you understand his importance in your organization and, indeed, in your life.

Because most people don't do this, most distributors feel isolated and alone. They're never quite sure what to do, never know what to expect from you, or even what's available. In short order, they're disillusioned, and then, in the wink of an eye, they're on to something else, impoverishing you and limiting your opportunities.

Don't let this happen to you. Tell your distributor up front just how important he is to you. Make it clear that you'll do your part to bolster and build this relationship, but that you have a right to expect him to do his.

▍ Make Sure Each Distributor Has A Realistic Plan

I've already discussed the importance of realistic planning. You must make sure each of your distributors has such a plan, that it's realistic, and that you're going to do your part to help the distributor achieve the objective. I see absolutely nothing wrong with asking each of your distributors for a monthly copy of this plan. You won't get it, of course, but there's no harm in asking.

Why won't you get it from most distributors? Because they'll offer a million excuses why it's neither possible to plan nor provide you with a copy of their plan. This is ridiculous!

Setting a realistic objective and creating a realistic plan for achieving it is at the heart of network marketing success. Part of your value to your new recruits is the experience you bring to the table. This experience enables you to assess whether any individual plan is realistic given the kinds of resources the recruit has available.

Yes, you'll probably find it difficult to get all your distributors to plan, much less share your plans with you, but ask anyway. The best candidates will comply and in their compliance is your enhanced success.

▍ Talk To Your Independent Distributors At Regular Intervals

If you want to succeed in network marketing, you must institute and maintain regular communication with all members of your organization. The purpose of such communication is to:

- familiarize yourself with their strengths, weaknesses
- ascertain and assess their plans
- find out what's working for them and what isn't in terms of both independent distributor recruitment and retention
- provide necessary technical assistance
- fine tune everything they do and provide the benefit of your considerable experience.

Do you do this now? Well, most upline sponsors don't. Somehow the disastrous notion has taken root in this industry that it's unnecessary to maintain substantive contact with downline members. Perhaps this is because laziness is the norm in this industry and good habits are at a discount. But you must be different.

You're got to run your organization as if you were the national sales manager of a company whose success depended on the success of dozens, hundreds, even thousands of independent field distributors. It's your job, sales manager, to

- keep complete distributor records, including name, address, phone, fax, *etc*.
- record data which may be pertinent for assisting each distributor (such as when and how to contact, best times for contacting, times distributor isn't available, *etc*.)
- initiate contact; it's not your job to wait to hear from your field force... it's your job to get in touch with them to find out what you need to know;
- constantly think up ways of helping your field force and bring these ways to their attention.

Put like this, I trust you can see just how remiss the directors of sales and marketing are at virtually all network marketing companies. The last, the very last thing, they consider is how to improve the productivity of their field force. Indeed, most of them are as disconnected from the reality and support of their field forces as the Court of Versailles was from the peasants of 18th century France. And, indeed, these directors of marketing, whatever they may say to the contrary, maintain the same thinly veiled contempt for their distributors which the aristos maintained. Yet we all know what happened to *them*!

A well-run network marketing company should maintain its focus on just three things:

- keeping its product line on the cutting edge so that it cannot be outmaneuvered by better-placed competitors;

- administering the company effectively so that there are neither financial nor personnel problems and that all the routine matters of any company are taken care of promptly and efficiently, and

- doing everything possible to sustain the independent distributor.

As you already know, this is *not* the way network marketing companies think. Their focus is all too often on draining as much money as possible from the entity as soon as possible; on recruiting independent distributors and squeezing all the money from them as quickly as they can… then letting the chips fall where they may. Coming up with a thorough-going, considered, productive distributor plan is far, far from their thoughts.

Which is why you've got to take on this task.

The minute you've sponsored even one distributor is the minute you need to adopt your newest, and arguably most important role, that of hands-on sales manager. You can no longer afford to wait for the company to act… you can no longer afford to wail about the inadequacies of the company… you can no longer afford the kind of bovine optimism that distinguishes the vast majority of people in network marketing. All these moods and responses are now inappropriate. If the company won't play out its appropriate role as lifeline to its distributor force, why then, my embryonic MLM millionaire, you're going to have to do so yourself!

This means instituting regular communication with *each* distributor. Schedule a set time at least every two weeks with each of your distributors. Half an hour should be enough time. Ask each distributor to call you and report. During this time find out:

- what kind of lead prospecting the distributor is doing

- how many self-mailers have been sent out

- what kinds of ads the distributor is placing; whether he is using his Ad-Net space-ad certificates

- whether he has qualified and closed his Ad-Net leads

- what other sources of leads he's assessing; whether he's putting together needed ad co-ops.

- how his telephone qualifying and closing skills are progressing, and of course

- how many people he's closed and whether he's assisting them get off to a good start.

So standard are these questions that you should list them in a computer file and just call up the screen as your conversation starts.

What you should be listening for is evidence that this distributor is approaching the task of organization recruitment and maintenance in a rigorous, organized fashion — or whether it's hit or miss, helter-skelter, vague, disorganized, inefficient. If the former, you should spend the bulk of your time on actual cases and on refining the overall method to make it more efficient still. If the latter, it's your responsibility to find out when the distributor intends to get started, what the problem is, when he's going to commit not only time and money… but organizational energy to getting the job done.

You must remind him what your expectations are… you must let him know that you, too, only have limited time and resources; that you want to be helpful but that you've got to see evidence of improvement. You must let him know you won't tolerate the inefficient and inept in your organization… and that inefficiency and ineptness won't help him reach his goal, either. In short, you must evidence willingness to assist but intolerance of poor habits.

Leave this person with a distinct list of tasks to be accomplished by your next meeting time, tasks such as so many leads to be pre-qualified, so many leads to be called, so many self-mailers to be sent, so many ads to be placed, *etc.* People who are going to succeed in network marketing love having these kinds of goals and the kind of discipline that enables such goals to be met. The also-rans detest them, always claiming that such discipline limits their freedom and never finding it difficult to offer "reasons" why they can't be so efficient.

Maintaining this kind of regular communication takes work. It may well be that you're currently working a full-time job, that when you come home you're not only tired but have family responsibilities to attend to. That your responsibilities so fill both your evenings and week-ends that there is precious little additional time. It's because there is so precious little additional time, friend, that you've got to make these communications sessions pay off.

- Schedule your meetings at regular intervals;
- Have an agenda. Don't talk aimlessly. Know what you want to accomplish; then make sure you do accomplish it;
- Summarize the meeting findings and results. Don't be afraid to point out what the independent distributor is doing right… and what he should do more of. By the same token, be clear about what he's not doing right and what he must do to achieve superior results. It does no one a favor, neither you nor the distributor, to hold anything back. Praise promising and substantial results. Make suggestions and get the independent contractor to agree to how to do better.

There is nothing glamorous in the work of regular follow-up and communication. It is, however, essential to your success. Commit yourself to it. And follow through religiously.

▮ Make Leads Available

It should be apparent to you by now just how important I regard the maintenance of a regular flow of prospect leads. And not just for yourself… but for all members of your organization.

This is not, unfortunately, the way most people in network marketing think. No indeed. There are any number of witless individuals masquerading as marketers in this business who just don't get it. In this connection, I talked to a fellow the other day who flatly disowned any responsibility for assisting members of his organization to get the leads they need. "I have enough leads for myself," he told me, "that's all I need to worry about."

The pompous ass!

That most assuredly was NOT all he had to worry about.

Even if you are fortunate enough to have regular sources of prospect leads, it's your responsibility to assist members of your organization secure prospect leads, too. Nor is this at all altruistic. Network marketing organizations grow because prospect leads are constantly suffused through all levels of the organization, because all members of the organization have a steady source of leads. Leads, dear reader, are like blood to the body. It isn't enough for just the head to have blood… the arms, legs, fingers, and toes must have blood, too… or the entire body suffers.

Just why this point is so difficult for so many people in network marketing to grasp puzzles me. I think it's because the resolutely team nature of network marketing is not widely known or appreciated. If you go into network marketing for yourself, you will lose. If you think your own success is all that matters, you will effectively curtail that success and make it impossible.

Like many people new to network marketing I did not grasp this point sufficiently well when I first signed up. I built my organization ever more widely… but not down. I figured that if I could build my first line so easily, they could certainly build theirs. But this was wrong.

Fortunately, however, I learned. And as I learned, I turned my attention ever more completely to the business of generating prospect leads. It was when I understood that it was my job, as national sales manager of my organization, to promote the well-being of my field force that I:

- joined Ad-Net and required members of my organization to do so so that they would have at least 30 leads per month;

- began aggressively creating card-deck and other ad co-ops;

- put together a space-ad co-op program fueled by the monthly Ad-Net certificates, *etc.*

As soon as I started doing these things, more and more leads became available to members of my organization. By working the kinds of techniques recommended in this book, my independent distributors closed more and still more of these prospects so that my organizations experienced the sustained growth which continues today. That is why I insist that *all* members of my organizations do everything possible to maximize their available sources of prospect leads.

During your regular reporting sessions, you must make sure your prospects are also maximizing their available sources. Find out by asking about:

- **Ad-Net membership.** Has your independent distributor joined Ad-Net yet? Why not? The Ad-Net membership cost is modest, and you need to do only a limited amount of recruiting (just two people!) to make it self-financing.

- **card-deck co-ops.** Make sure to create a card-deck co-op for your opportunity and enlist each of your distributors so that they get leads on a regular basis. **Note**: call me right away to see if the space is available for your opportunity in my card-deck. And don't forget, as a card-deck broker, I can place your card for lower cost in all other decks. In short, make *me* a partner in your card-deck lead-generating plans.

- **space-ad co-ops.** If you're in Ad-Net, of course, you receive each month a free certificate. Gather all these certificates together from members of your organization. Give them and your camera-ready ad copy to Dr. Robert Davidson, and he'll be happy to place these ads for you and generate still more prospect leads.

- **other lead-generator programs.** Don't forget bingo cards. You can get members of your organization to purchase leads from me through my Nationwide Lead-Generator program. This is another good way of generating thousands of leads annually which your distributors can work for their benefit — and yours!

Let me be very clear about this: you cannot succeed in network marketing unless you give sustained attention to developing ongoing prospect lead sources. In this connection, I think, for instance, of a fellow I know in Vermont who's been "working" network marketing for many years now — but unsuccessfully so. One reason why this obstinate slug is so unsuccessful is because he can come up with millions of good "reasons" why he can't assist his organization develop their lead sources. As a result, he always has inadequate sources of leads. But when you limit your leads, it's just like limiting the amount of blood that flows to the brain. You feel faint... and in short order you pass out, entirely unable to function. This is the habitual condition of this poor creature: blacked out. Long ago, of course, I realized he was a hopeless case. Now I am utterly contemptuous of him in all dealings. I realize he is one of the uneducables.

But not you: YOU realize just how important lead sources are... and as you talk to members of your downline, I feel confident you are going to both quiz and push so they do what's necessary to keep the maximum number of prospect leads flowing through your organization!!!

■ **Develop A Group Newsletter**

As your organization grows first into the dozens, then into the hundreds, finally into the thousands of members you are just not going to be able to keep in touch with them all by phone. This is the condition I am in *vis à vis* my organizations... and I know what I'm talking about. Even if three or four people call you for advice daily, you're still not going to be able to assist even a small fraction of your burgeoning organization. Prepare for this day as soon as possible!

When I entered the network marketing business, I had no idea that I was shortly to be in the newsletter business, too, but this, I quickly came to realize, was an inevitability. If I wanted the people in my organization to be regularly instructed in my marketing procedures, a newsletter was a necessity... not least because your people are just not going to be able to get marketing assistance from the publications put out by the parent company.

Before going on, grab the last issue of your company's publication. Is this publication dedicated to publishing articles which tell you how to:

- generate leads
- identify prospects
- close prospects
- develop and maintain a productive organization
- run successful space ads
- use card-decks for your benefit, *etc.*, *etc.*, *etc.*?

Of course not!

The idiots in your front office are the same as the idiots in the front offices of all the network marketing companies. They focus their publications on...

- trivia about people in the front office (have you noticed how often they'll run shots of secretaries or the boys on the loading dock?)
- what the president's been doing lately
- the new products the company's added
- glowing testimonials about how well everybody is doing... without giving you step-by-step details on how it happened.

You already know that the network marketing companies are derelict in their duty to you, the independent distributor. So why should it be any different when they sit down to plan their newsletters and other periodical publications? Here, too, they evidence the same glaring lack of concern for distributor welfare that they show in all their other dealings. **Note**: Here I must give credit to Don Smyth of The Staff of Life, Bill Blaesing of The Gourmet Coffee Club and Ed Freeman of The World's Largest Permanent Downline. All recognize the importance of providing their members with useful, ongoing marketing information; the kind of information you're getting in this resource. Each asked me to help provide such information, and I do, monthly. That's right: every 30 days I provide up-to-date information to all members of the company on what they can do — right now! — to recruit and retain members and so make more money. Tell your company CEO to call me; the people in your company could use this tailored, specific information, too!

If your company isn't providing or won't provide this kind of information, YOU, despite all the other things you've got to do, have got to become a newsletter publisher, too. Because you need to disseminate crucial marketing information to assist your members... and because you cannot expect the company, with all its lofty disdain for the mundane realities of wealth building, to help you.

Here's what you've got to do.

- Appoint yourself publisher.
- Brainstorm some names for your new publication.
- Determine what's going to be in it. Here are the kind of features people want to know about:
    - tips on sponsoring new members
    - tips on retaining members
    - marketing tips in all areas
    - lead generating
    - successful methods being utilized by members of the team
    - telemarketing advice
    - direct mail advice
    - updates on company and other marketing materials.

In short, leave the company to handle all product-related matters in its publication. Make yours devoted solely to marketing and organizational development advice.

- Figure out the financing. Even a short two- or four-page monthly newsletter costs money. Costs include:

- paper
- printing
- envelopes
- first-class postage.

Who's going to pay for this? Well, you either have to pay for it yourself, or assess your organization's members a small annual fee, like $10. That should be enough to pay for a year's "subscription." Too, there's another way of cutting costs. Distribute it on a "first line" basis. You send the newsletter to distributors on your first line; let them distribute it to people on their first line, *etc*. This will only work, however, if all parties recognize their responsibility to copy and distribute the newsletter promptly. Unfortunately, they don't always do so.

Resource & Tribute

To give you some idea what the marketing tips section of a company newsletter should look like, I've reproduced two pages from a recent Staff of Life newsletter. You see how specific and detailed they are? Also, even though I provide these kinds of marketing tips monthly for The Staff of Life newsletter, my partner Robert Blackman also produces a bi-monthly "update" newsletter, packed with still more marketing details, and available only to members of our fast-growing organization. Producing this detailed, helpful newsletter is a lot of work, yet Robert does so willingly, knowing it's all for the good of our team. I take this opportunity to pay warm tribute to Robert for all all his hard work for the general good. No one knows better than I both the cost of doing so — or how helpful it is. If you'd like to see a couple of samples of his fine distributor marketing and update newsletter, send Robert $3.

Member Q & A

Q - I've got a nice growing organization in The Staff of Life now. I've reached my initial goal of paying for my family's own products and I've decided I want to earn at least $1,000 per month by this time next year. Can you give me some help on achieving my objective?

A - Thanks for writing. We're glad you're already doing so well, and we're happy to take this opportunity to help you do even better. Here is a list of things that can help:

1) Write down your objective in the form of a promise or contract with yourself. "I promise myself to do what is necessary to reach an income in The Staff of Life of at least $1,000 per month by June 1, 1996." Then date and sign it, just like you would any important paper.

2) Post this objective where you can see it every day. Carry it in your wallet... or pocket. Put in on the refrigerator door. Look at it first thing in the morning, last thing at night. What you're doing is training your mind. Specific objectives are actually quite easy to reach so long as they're precise. As renowned Georgia Tech football coach Homer Rise used to say, "I write down by goals on 3 x 5 cards, one on each card. I take them with me everywhere. When I'm at the airport waiting for a plane, I'll pull them out and begin to read them. The real fun is expecting them to happen." Exactly!

3) Figure out what you need to do to reach your objective.

To reach an income of $1,000 a month here is one possible scenario...

Since the average monthly purchase per Distributor is around $100, we'll assume at least $60 each. And since different percentages are paid on the different levels, the following might show how an income of $1,000 per month could be reached:

Number of Distributors		Monthly Purchase			Commission
Level 1	4	$60	5%	=	$12
Level 2	16	$60	5%	=	$48
Level 3	32	$60	10%	=	$192
Level 4	84	$60	15%	=	$756
		Total			$1,008

This does not included any bonuses that might be earned from people on your 5th and 6th levels.

4) List all the tasks that need to be done to reach your objective.

During any given month, here are the things that need to happen so that you can reach your objective:

- identify a certain number of prospects;
- call or talk to these prospects to ensure that they're interested in better health and a solid business opportunity;
- make sure all these prospects get detailed information on The Staff of Life and our products;
- follow up with a phone call or subsequent visit to discuss the company, its products, what they are doing for you, and to make sure that all the prospect's questions are answered.
- sign up new recruits and help them place the product order that makes most sense for them.

This is what you've got to do to recruit new people in any given month.

You've also got to consider what the people in your organization are doing and provide them with needed assistance. Thus,

- keep complete records of the names, addresses, and phone numbers of all the people in your organization, keeping particular note of the people on your first line;
- review the month report provided by the company to see which of these are both recruiting new people and purchasing product, and which ones are not;
- send congratulatory notes of encouragement to the people who are developing productive organizations;
- call people in your organization who are either not recruiting or not purchasing product to find out what you can do to help. Is there a reason why they've not participating? When do they intend to start participating fully?

What can you do to help them?

5) At the end of every 14 days, review your performance to see how you're doing.

If you're going to make at least $1,000 a month within one year, each day counts. Each day you either make progress towards your objective, or you don't. There is no other possibility. You want to make sure that you're being as productive as possible. Thus,

- review your contacts with prospects and people already in your organization. Were you as productive as you could be? Did you know the answers to questions you were asked? If not, have you taken steps so you'll know them next time? If you didn't know the answers yourself, did you know what to do? Did you know who to refer the questions to for proper handling?

Note: We at headquarters are always ready to assist you in answering your prospects' questions or in talking to your prospects personally. Call us at 509-738-2345 for assistance.

- Were you able to answer people's product questions fully and accurately? If not, have you scheduled some time for yourself to become better acquainted with what The Staff of Life makes available?

- Did you return people's phone calls and answer their letters promptly so as to expedite your business? If not, can you rearrange your schedule so that you'll have the time you need to run this aspect of your business more efficiently?

- Did you have all the prospects you need? To succeed in growing your Staff of Life business, you're going to need a regular supply of prospects. If you have your own sources, fine. If not, the company can assist you.

- You can run space ads in publications of your own choosing. The Staff of Life has many company-approved ads. These are available by calling Robert Blackman at Diversified Enterprises, (405) 360-9487.

- Do you have the marketing communications that you need? Like any business The Staff of Life uses a number of marketing communications to ensure that its message and products are properly presented. The basic marketing communication is our company 'self-mailer'. All you have to do is address it and pop on a 32 cent postage stamp and it's ready to go. It contains the basic information people need to know about our products, the company, our philosophy, and way of doing business.

Important note: The Staff of Life self-mailer has just been updated to include details about all our new products and the difference they make in people's lives. Your prospects will want to know about both these products and how they can help them. The self-mailer tells them just what they need to know. To get your self-mailers, contact Robert Blackman at Diversified Enterprises (405) 360-9487. Each self-mailer can be personalized with your name, address, phone and fax number and company i.d. We firmly believe that no other company offers such complete information about itself and products in such an easy-to-use form. This is the marketing communication you want to use when you want your prospects to know -- in detail -- the products we offer and the benefits they create.

After you review your performance, make the necessary adjustments. A business is an organic thing. It doesn't run on automatic pilot. You've got to plan what to do... work your plan... and review your results -- all on a regular basis.

If you don't like what you see at the end of each fourteen day period, don't condemn yourself. Just make the necessary adjustments and carry on. Fortunately, you're representing a company and products that people really benefit from and want to know about. They're going to help you! Just keep in touch with them and give them what they ask for... then follow up to make sure they've followed through, signed up, purchased product, etc.

6) Keep a chart noting your progress.

Whether you're using a computer or just a notebook to record your business data, make sure to develop a chart that has the following categories:

Month
Number or People in Your Organization
Group Volume
Commission
Percentage Increase Over Previous Month

By reviewing this chart, you're able to

- determine if you're reaching (or not reaching) your monthly objectives
- see which months were best for you and, by reviewing your notes, determine why
- equally, see which months were worst for you and by reviewing your notes and subsequent performance, make sure you've determined the reasons and corrected them
- see if your organization is growing at a steady, measured pace and project six months or a year ahead, thereby giving yourself a sense of where you're going to be... whether that makes you happy, or whether you're going to have to step up the pace to meet your objectives.

In short, this chart, with its essential data, provides you with crucial information for making your business as successful as you want it to be.

7) If you fall behind one month, don't get discouraged and beat yourself up. Do the best you can with what you have now.

For whatever reason, people occasionally have to take some time off to attend to family problems, because of personal illness, or even to rest and reflect. That's natural. What's important, however, is not to let this state continue indefinitely. Just because you haven't been able to run your business at 100% efficiency, doesn't mean you shouldn't run it at all!

The important thing is that if you stop, take the time you need... but then start again. Go back to the beginning of this article and read through it carefully, setting your objective, plotting your steps to achieving it. Don't let a temporary hiatus become a permanent drag on your success. That just doesn't make sense!

8) Take the long view.

We all know the expression that "Rome wasn't built in a day." But some of us forget that this doesn't just apply to great cities but to significant enterprises of every kind. The people who are successful in The Staff of Life work at developing their organizations day in, day out. Sure, like all people, they have days which are better, and some which aren't. What's important, however, is that when they have a very good day, they don't just sit on their laurels thinking they've reached the pinnacle of success. They carry on, knowing that even better days are coming. By the same token if they have a bad batch, they don't moan that they've come to the end of their rope and give up. No, they carry on. Get the message?

The world now contains upwards to 7 billion people. Although we at The Staff of Life have touched the lives of literally hundreds of thousands of people, we still have billions and billions of people to connect with, inform about our products, get them started taking charge of their health, get them off to a good start in launching their businesses, and generally assisting. This isn't going to take a month, a year, or even a decade. It's the work of a lifetime.

In this context, therefore, the people who are doing the best in The Staff of Life have done certain important things which are worth sharing with others who want to be equally successful:

- they have made a lifelong commitment to their own better health and the better health of the people they care about;
- they have determined which Staff of Life products make the most sense for them... and for their families;
- they have made a lifetime commitment to ensuring that they bring these products and their benefits to the attention of the largest number of people possible;
- they have set up plans of different durations for achieving their personal and professional goals insofar as they relate to The Staff of Life and our products. These different time lines include 1 month plans, six month plans, one year plans, three year plans, etc.
- having planned their work, they work their plans, making sure that the utmost number of days possible are profitable days, days where objectives were reached and where progress was made to longer-term objectives.

These people -- and we have an increasing number of them with the company -- know that success is achieved a day at a time, and they are working daily to achieve it. Given what you've shared with us about yourself, your belief in our products, and enthusiasm for the task ahead, we feel sure in one year you'll be making at least $1,000 a month from your Staff of Life organization. Be sure to keep us informed of your progress so we can congratulate you as you grow!

■ Prod The Company To Publicize Your Group's Successes

Organizations begin to roll along when prospects get the sense that all is going well in the organization, that people are making money. They want to be part of the successful organization. Apt use of the company's publication helps create this sense not only about the company but more particularly about your organization within the company.

- Make it a point to use the company's publications. It's amazing to me just how few distributors are actually ever mentioned in the company's publications. Why? Perhaps they don't feel worthy! Well, if this is you GET OVER IT! The company's publication exists, in my view, to publicize you and your organization. It is your job to create news... and to get this news publicized in the company's publications. Why, pick up any issue of The Staff of Life, Gourmet Coffee Club, and Ad-Net publications and you'll find — me. Me! My organization! Our successes! We want to provide a sense of movement and success... and in every issue we do!!!

- Brainstorm story ideas. Anything relating to your group can and should be publicized in the company's publications. Has one of your group members achieved notable sales results? Publish it. Has one of your group members just had a baby? Publish that. Has one of your members come up with an unusual sales tip or technique? Publish that. In short, brainstorm all possible story ideas and make sure to bring them to the attention of the editor.

- Know the editor and stay in touch. Editors need material for their publications. And all editors like to have sources... people they can go to at a moment's notice, knowing they'll be rewarded with something they can publish. Be this person! Write the editor a letter, introduce yourself, say that you've got a fast-growing group with lots of people with lots of interesting information. Tell the editor you'll be happy to submit this information on a regular basis... and provide him with your phone number so he can get to you, too, if he has some space to fill. Then be as good as your word: collect your data... and keep in touch.

- Tell members of your organization through *your* newsletter to glean news items of interest. Tell them what you're looking for and urge them to submit this information directly to you for transmittal to the editor.

- Advise members of your organization to get photographs of themselves. Company magazines should promote company people. This includes both news items... and photographs. Don't wait until you need these photographs (when you might find you don't have anything suitable). Tell your group members to find photographs now.

- Make sure all members of your organization are publicized as members of your organization. Remember, you want to create a sense of excitement, of movement about your team. The best way to do this is to ensure that when anyone is mentioned they're specifically cited as a member of your team. Thus, when members of your organization are mentioned in the company publication, the caption should read something like this, "/name of person publicized or photographed/, a member of /name of your organization/". This is good promotion for the member of your team, of course, and good promotion, too, for your team overall. **Note**: Don't be surprised if the company gets queasy about this. While they're all in favor of team effort in theory, when your team starts rockin' and rollin' and its members are constantly in the publication, they'll start worrying... They'll start talking about how they can't give all this publicity just to one team... how you've got to remember they're are others in the company, that it's not fair to give all the publicity to you. What they really mean, of course, is that they're nervous that you'll be perceived as the company, that people will think no one else is doing anything (despite the fact that that's the truth), and that you'll have to understand they must do something for everyone. This, of course, is ridiculous! The people who do the work, who brainstorm ideas, who come up with the photographs, who know, in short, how to use the publication to their benefit, should be the ones who get the coverage — and damn the rest.

Last Words On Sustaining Your Team

By following these steps you'll find your organization growing by leaps and bounds. Congratulations. You are now benefiting from the essence of multi-level marketing: finding good people and helping you both profit by helping your people replicate their efforts and produce benefits for everyone. You deserve all the rewards you're now certain to get.

Don't blow it!

You've moved to the top of your company by following these sensible steps. Now you've got to stay there by maintaining them. The problem is that as you grow you're going to have less and less time... with more and more responsibilities. Welcome to the major problem of success in America: balancing all your responsibilities so that you can ensure the continuation and indeed development of your success.

In this connection,

- use your publication to tell your downline members when's the best time to call. Start making better use of "scrap time" to stay in touch. Have people call Friday evening, Saturday morning or Sunday afternoon. These tend to be quiet times in most people's lives.

- Have them fax in their questions so you can get them an answer at your leisure.

- Tell people to think through their questions before they call you. Having thought through their questions, do they really need to call you? Isn't the information they need available in either your materials or those supplied by the company? (In this connection I'm thinking of a fellow who called me last week to ask a question about a grocery coupon program. I told him I knew nothing about that and provided him with the name and phone number of the company's liaison, the person who handles this matter. But just yesterday he called again to ask the same question. He didn't get a very civil reception, believe me. I expect people to think about what they want, to be prepared to get the answer promptly, and to get off the phone as soon as possible.)

- Tell people to be prepared when they call you. They shouldn't keep you waiting while they search for a pen that works or a piece of paper. You're entirely right to chastise people who are so ineptly organized. Their time may not be valuable, but, believe me, as your organization balloons up into the thousands, yours is.

- Explain that you like to keep all calls to not more than three minutes in length. When I was a teen-ager, garrulous like most of my peers, my father used to time my calls to ensure they were never more than 3 minutes in length. It galled then, but today, older, I see the utility and abide by it. You'll find that you can deal with most matters with conversations of not more than 180 seconds. Lots of people in network marketing are phone-freaks, perfectly happy to spend hours on the phone, saying nothing. Don't make this mistake. If people are organized when they call you, you can be organized in handling their business.

Note: when you become as organized as this, I warn you that many people in network marketing will find you brusque and unfriendly. Because they are accustomed to passing the time of day in their calls, they'll find your focused approach to business unorthodox, unnerving, approaching rudeness. If so, use your newsletter to define your approach to distributor relations and let people know precisely what you expect from them... and precisely what you're going to do. If there are no surprises for the loquacious distributors, there should be less criticism.

One Last Thing: Making Sure Everyone In Your Organization Has A Copy Of This Resource

We are now approaching the end of the most sensible book ever written on network marketing. When you follow its guidelines, you'll prosper. When your entire organization follows its guidelines, you'll prospect even faster. Thus, draw the obvious deduction: make sure each member of your organization gets and studies this book.

- Call me about buying books by the case. If you've got a substantial organization, I'm happy to sell you books wholesale. You can sell them directly to your people and profit in two ways — through the sale of the book itself and by helping them build more profitable organizations.

- Ask each person in your organization to send me $25.95 and where they'd like the book shipped.

- Call or fax me a list of the names/addresses of all people in your organization. I'll be happy to send a free year's subscription to my quarterly Sure-Fire Business Success catalog, along with complete details on this resource. You can tell people through your newsletter to expect it.

- Tell your company about this resource. I am more than happy to provide a bulk sale to a company at a discounted price and to work with them to provide sales materials, order forms, *etc*. Indeed, I'm even prepared to go farther: depending on how many copies the company might buy I'll do a special edition of this book just for your company, with, perhaps, a special preface by your company's president. That's right! I can put a special preface by you or your company president here featuring your own words to motivate your people.

- Further, I am willing to provide a review copy of this book to the editor of any network marketing publication, including company newsletters and publications. Editors may thus tell readers about this book, so long as they're willing to publicize its price and order details. More, I am happy to give my permission to have this book excerpted so that all distributors can learn about the techniques they should be using to achieve success.

I am, in short, willing to work with anyone in network marketing to ensure that all independent distributors in this backward industry get the crucial information they need to succeed. Help me!

Note: in this connection, my Sure-Fire Business Success columns are also available to company publications. I am happy to send a complete inventory of all the columns, most of which are appropriate for network marketers. There is no charge to run these articles, so long as the "Resource Box" which runs with each article is published. This box contains order details for some of my books and materials, including prices, address and phone. To receive a listing of available articles, just call me.

If you want to work with me, I'm more than ready to work with you!

CONCLUSION

The first stage of our time together is now over. Now it's time for you to go out and follow these steps to build your organization on all levels, whatever MLM opportunity you're in.

Fortunately, our road need not part here. Not by a long shot. I'm ready, willing and able to help you make increasing amounts of money each month. Here's how we can work together:

1) If you're happy with the MLM company you're in, then let me help you make it a bigger success. Call me today to reserve either 50,000 or 100,000 cards in my next quarterly Sales & Marketing Success Deck.

2) If you don't have the money for at least 50,000 cards and can't yet put together a co-op (you should be trying, you know), then take a 60-character ad on the lead-generator card in the same quarterly card deck. This is a good way for you to start getting leads promptly. Then plan to upgrade to a full card as soon as you can.

3) Join my Ad-Net organization and make sure all the people in your organization do the same. You know why I recommend Ad-Net and you know why it works. So, join me... and start getting the maximum number of prospect leads into the hands of all people in your organization so that you can leverage faster growth.

4) Bring the L.A.N.T. System to the attention of the CEO of your company. Let me tell you something: the L.A.N.T. System means big money for the company using it. We know. We have a mile of data now from the companies successfully using it. Our goal with this System is a simple one: to increase the likelihood of profit for every individual distributor. We're not interested in how things are done in any company; we're only interested in maximizing the return for all the independent distributors. And we review everything with that single standard in mind. If the CEO of your company really has this objective, too, we want to talk to him/her.

5) If the CEO won't use our system and you feel that the company marketing materials aren't sufficiently client-centered (a good bet), then call me today and take advantage of the trained copywriters at my National Copywriting Center. I can help you produce any marketing communications you need in reasonable time at reasonable cost.

6) Review the additional materials in Appendix II to see what else I've got to help. If you didn't get this book directly from me, call to get a free year's subscription to my quarterly Sure-Fire Business Success Catalog. I'm always adding new things to help. My brain didn't stop when I wrote this book; yours shouldn't stop, either, when you've read it.

7) Finally, if you come to the conclusion that you're not going to make money in any network marketing company you're in, join me. I'm looking for effective, professional, dedicated, hard-working people who will work with me to make us both a continuing, growing monthly profit. Just complete any or all of the applications in this book and you'll hear from me promptly with detailed marketing guidelines and regular updates on how to make money in network marketing, just as I've outlined in this book.

In short, take action.

I know now it's possible to make substantial amounts of money in network marketing. And I've worked hard to perfect the system that turns the possible into the actual. Every day I work this system, and so do the get-ahead members of my teams in the various opportunities I both endorse and work.

Every day, too, I let the industry dinosaurs who still exist in such vast numbers know that their sloth, disorganization, self-defeating behaviors, contemptuous behavior and selfish rapaciousness are no longer acceptable.

Thus, I approach each day with twin missions: to help members of my teams prosper faster and to a greater extent... and to continue my exhilarating fight against the backward bumpkins of this so often despicable "industry."

Join me. Use these techniques to enrich yourself and members of your success teams. Bring these techniques to the attention of your CEOs and industry leaders. Make them show you that they value your success by showing you what specifically they are doing to help you achieve it. And if they won't show you (as so many will not), then join my growing commando band and find personal profit and the sense of doing well by doing good.

No, friend, our time together doesn't end here. It begins. Today we are the resistance. Tomorrow the citadel is ours. I know. Since I first wrote this book thousands of people now know what to do to achieve success... Many are either pushing their slothful companies to reform... or have made the decision to leave such companies to join me. Good for them. And good for you because, you see, you're now the next one who's been trained to help both yourself and the members of your soon-to-be burgeoning organization.

ABOUT THE AUTHOR: DR. JEFFREY LANT

Millions of business people around the world now rely on the sensible, hard-hitting, eminently practical business information provided by Dr. Jeffrey Lant.

Over 200 publications and electronic data bases worldwide now carry his "Sure-Fire Business Success" and "Qwik Smarts by Dr. Jeffrey Lant" columns.

Another million a year read his quarterly Sure-Fire Business Success Catalog.

A different 100,000 receive his Sales & Marketing Success Deck every 90 days.

Since entering network marketing, he's become the #1 distributor in two companies, Ad-Net and The Gourmet Coffee Club, and head of the fastest-growing organization in a 3rd, The Staff of Life. He and his partner Robert Blackman are always ready to assess new business opportunities that conform to his rigorous standards for assisting the independent distributor achieve and maintain success.

He's the author of 12 books, including such well known titles as **Cash Copy: How To Offer Your Products And Services So Your Prospects Buy Them Now; The Unabashed Self-Promoter's Guide: What Every Man, Woman, Child And Organization In America Needs To Know About Getting Ahead By Exploiting The Media; Money Talks: The Complete Guide To Creating A Profitable Workshop Or Seminar In Any Field**, and **How To Make A Whole Lot More Than $1,000,000 Writing, Commissioning, Publishing And Selling 'How-To' Information**. When Jeffrey writes a book, he sets out with a single mission: to make it the standard resource in the field, the benchmark against which all other books in that field are compared.

Personally, Jeffrey is an avid art collector collecting Old Master paintings from the 17th through 19th centuries. Having earned four college degrees (including a Ph.D. from Harvard), he is also holder of four titles of ancient nobility dating back to the Third Crusade. As such his proper title is "His Highness The Prince of Tornavan."

Unique among authors, Jeffrey Lant's direct-access telephone number runs with every book, catalog, article, card-deck, and audio cassette, easily making him the world's most reachable author and business authority.

You can call him right now at (617) 547-6372. Just be ready to do business!

APPENDIX I

HOW TO LEVERAGE YOUR NETWORK MARKETING BUSINESS THROUGH AD-NET

The network marketing community is divided into two parts. The larger part approaches the business of MLM as if this were 1900 and people were still using horses and buggies. They approach one person at a time... talking to them at length on the phone, scheduling one-on-one meetings, going to their homes and offices... in short engaging in a series of acts designed to ensure the expenditure of the most resources for the least result.

The other kind of people, unfortunately still the minority, understand that network marketing is about leverage... about getting the largest number of people to see your message and engage the largest number of people to join and become productive members of your team.

Your first decision is to decide which team you're going to join...

Personally, I've made my decision: I want to use the greatest amount of leverage possible to recruit the largest number of people possible in the shortest possible time and so instruct these people so that they, in turn, can recruit the greatest number of people in the shortest period of time. This, you see, is the real way to riches in network marketing.

If this is the decision you've made, pay real close attention since the means are at hand for staggering growth in your organization. Here's how it works:

- Join Ad-Net. You already know what Ad-Net is and what it does. It's the best of the crop of prospect-generating network marketing companies on the market, not perfect, but entirely serviceable for our needs.

- Use your monthly allotment of Ad-Net leads. Each month Ad-Net sends you 30, 50 or 100 names of potential members of your organization, people looking for a solid, profitable business opportunity. To start, call these people and ask them the tough pre-qualifying questions I've recommended in the text. Your job is to find out if they're really looking for a solid opportunity and will work with you to develop their business. If they won't, write them off. If they will, work with them, without entirely abandoning your skepticism about their intentions until you're quite convinced. **Note**: If the lead doesn't have a phone number, don't waste any time on this person. If you're feeling rich some month and simply want to send out some of your mailers, you can, but don't expect any return.

- If the people on your monthly Ad-Net lead list won't join your primary network marketing opportunity because they're working something else, don't worry. Just make sure to provide them with all the reasons why they'll be well off in your Ad-Net organization. (If you don't remember all the Ad-Net benefits, go back and reread the section starting on page 22 in this resource.)

- The minute you've got the prospect in Ad-Net, advise him/her to go into my card-deck (and, by extension, other card-decks in due course). Remember, you want this person to assemble co-ops using the money of people in his organization. Just ensure that each respondent is sent an Ad-Net self-mailer (available, as you know, through Robert Blackman at Diversified Enterprises at 405-360-9487) along with information on his primary MLM. This way you are starting to use *their* money to build *your* monthly Ad-Net check. **Note**: Make sure to get such co-ops going with *each* person you recruit who is working another MLM opportunity.

- Then, get your entire company to use The L.A.N.T. SYSTEM™. Contact Robert Blackman, P.O. Box 1390, Norman, OK 73070 and ask for a copy of The L.A.N.T. SYSTEM™ brochure and a cover letter you can send to your company CEO. This letter spells out the benefits of the System for the company. If the company signs up in Ad-Net, you'll be put directly underneath and all additional sign-ups can come under you. Please understand that this could be thousands and thousands of sign-ups depending on the size of the company. In short, for doing some easy networking, you could be cut in on a very substantial monthly income... but you've got to pre-sell your company CEO on the benefits of the System. (These benefits are clearly stated in the letter you'll send.) **Note**: You are not responsible for *closing* any deal with the company. We'll do that, so long as you let either Robert Blackman or me know just how things are coming along. We'll follow up promptly and appropriately. **Another note**: You are not limited to working with companies you belong to. You can work with members of your Ad-Net organization who belong to any network marketing company. You can assist one of your organization members send the L.A.N.T. SYSTEM™ details and cover letter to the CEO of his company, instructing him in how to pursue the matter. If the company buys the System, you and your partner can take a common share of Ad-Net and split the rewards equitably as you agree. This means you can work with literally dozens of people in presenting L.A.N.T. SYSTEM™ details to CEOs whose companies represent hundreds of thousands of independent distributors!

- Use your monthly Ad-Net free-ad coupons. As previously explained, you use these to generate more prospect leads. If you don't already have camera-ready ads, call me at (617) 547-6372 and let my National Copywriting Center produce them. As these leads come in, you'll close them, of course, into your Ad-Net organization... and network through people in other organizations to their CEOs as described above.

The L.A.N.T. SYSTEM™ involves leveraging from the top. You can, however, also leverage from the bottom and sides of an organization, thus:

- Sign up the newest, greenest, lowliest independent distributor in any network marketing company. Get this person to sponsor *his* upline sponsor in Ad-Net and then sponsor his entire downline, line by line, into Ad-Net. In this way, a clever person (even one at the bottom of the organizational heap) can quickly became a major network marketing player. **Note**: a person needn't be lowly and green, of course, to make a killing this way. You may take a person at any level of any MLM organization and help him recruit all members of his downline... and also his upline (and *his* downline), his *upline's* upline (and *his* downline), *etc., etc. etc.* until the entire company has been recruited.

In short, you must start looking at the tremendous networking potential of the person you are trying to recruit.

- Of course, you want to recruit him/her right away. That starts things off.
- Then you want to recruit his/her downline.
- Then his/her upline. And the upline's upline, as above.
- Then have this person do card-deck, lead-generating and space ad advertising.
- Then approach the CEO of his/her company to recruit the entire company.

You see, you must know precisely how you can profit from your new recruit once you've sponsored him/her. These linkages are like gold and must be used accordingly.

But, first, of course, you need to be in Ad-Net. For that, I've included an application form for you to complete. Before doing so, if you are already in network marketing, check with your upline to see if he/she is in my organization. Note, not just in Ad-Net... but in my Elite #1 Ad-Net Success Team. If the person is in Ad-Net but not in my Ad-

Net team, this situation can be rectified. To do so, call Ad-Net President Jim Wingo at (702) 227-6655. If this person is in both Ad-Net and my Success Team, then as a courtesy I urge you to let your current upline sponsor sponsor you.

If, however, this person is either in Ad-Net (but not in my organization) or still doesn't grasp the significance of the leveraging possibilities of Ad-Net, then by all means complete the application in this book. Keep a copy for yourself, and send completed application form and payment to Jim Wingo, President, Ad-Net, Inc. at 3227 Meade Ave. #3B, Las Vegas, NV 89102. If for some reason, the application form is not available, call me direct and I'll send one to you myself.

Once you're a member, follow these directions closely. This is the most clever leveraging scheme available in the whole of network marketing. And now it's available to you, wherever you're placed in your MLM opportunity.

APPENDIX II

RECOMMENDED RESOURCES & NETWORK MARKETING COMPANIES

■ **to produce your self-mailers (and any other kind of marketing communication)**

If you want self-mailers for your organization, we can write, design and print them. Start by calling me directly at (617) 547-6372 for complete details.

If you want other kinds of marketing communications (ads, flyers, brochures, cover letters, *etc*.), also call me. Network marketing communications are only a small part of our copywriting and printing business!

■ **for card-deck and other lead-generating mechanisms**

Contact Jeffrey Lant at (617) 547-6372. You can get 50,000 or 100,000 cards every 90 days in our Sales & Marketing Success Deck. Also, a 60-character ad on our Nationwide Lead-Generator card (goes to 100,000 prospects quarterly). We can also place your card in all other card decks for rates lower than you can get yourself. Remember, if you're not using card-decks to generate prospect leads, you're making a very significant error!

■ **for telemarketing assistance**

Want your prospect leads qualified to see which of them are worth bothering with? Contact Robert Blackman for information on our Tele-Close program or complete the application on page 142.

■ **to join Ad-Net**

Complete the application in this book on page 141 and return to Robert Blackman. If you have questions about how Ad-Net works, either reread the relevant pages in this book or call me.

■ **to produce computer diskettes for your program.**

If you want to put your company benefits and an application form on computer, contact George Kosch at Incor Publications, Suite 304, 11807-101 St., Edmonton, Alberta, T5G 2B6, Canada (403) 471-6308

■ **if you want to do network marketing in Canada**

Get George Kosch's informative guide to "Network Marketing in Canada." ($9.95 postpaid U.S.; $11.95 Canadian)

Special note for Canadian readers: I maintain active Canada-based teams for The Staff of Life, Gourmet Coffee Club, and Ad-Net. Call George Kosch for complete details. You'll be pleasantly surprised how much we have available to assist you!

■ **if you want to do network marketing in other countries**

Contact Jeffrey directly. We maintain success teams in many countries of the world and are more than happy to put you in touch with successful members of our teams abroad. Alternatively, we'll assist you get a team started wherever you are.

Useful MLM Videos To Assist You And Members Of Your Team

■ **Multi-Level Money Video**. Pop this 55-minute video into your VCR and catch the high spots of what it really takes to make money in MLM. This isn't one of those silly MLM cassettes produced by others where a bunch of nit-wits sit around telling dubious war stories about the money they've supposed made (but usually haven't). No, this is Jeffrey upclose and personal, being direct, candid, realistic and specific about what you've got to do to succeed in network marketing. #V2 VHS tape alone $33. #C10 V2 video tape + **Multi-Level Money book**. $45. (Save over $12.)

■ **Why I joined The Staff of Life... Why You Should Join, Too**. In this fast-moving 55-minute video, you'll learn why Jeffrey joined The Staff of Life, the substantial personal difference the company and its products have made for his health and well being, and how he has harnessed his marketing system to this superb company to create a universal money-making opportunity. If you're obese, suffer from constipation, gas, diarrhea, low energy, high blood pressure, high cholesterol, allergies, poor digestion (among many other conditions), you'll want to use The Staff of Life products just to feel better. If you're entrepreneurial, after viewing this video you'll see right away how you can make money in it. Give this tape to a prospect with one of our handy Staff of Life self-mailers, and you've got a sale. #V5 video. Just $25 postpaid.

Special Reports by Dr. Jeffrey Lant

Want to know more about specific subjects handled in this book? Then get your hands on Jeffrey's practical five-page computer-printed special reports, each one focusing on a specific topic with additional information.

#R103

WHAT YOU HAVE TO DO TO RETAIN YOUR MLM DOWNLINE. If you can't retain the people you recruit, you won't make money in MLM. Here's what you have to do so you will! $7

#R109

YOUR FIRST THIRTY DAYS IN NETWORK MARKETING, OR WHAT YOU'VE GOT TO DO TO GET OFF TO A SUCCESSFUL START Your first thirty days in network marketing provide a clear indication of whether you'll make money or just join the swollen ranks of MLM failures. Here are the precise things you've got to do to get yourself off to a profitable start. $7

#R110

HOW TO CLOSE YOUR MLM PROSPECTS ON THE PHONE. If you're going to make be a success in MLM, you've got to learn how to close prospects on the phone like we do in Tele-Close. This report tells you how! $7 (By the way, if you won't learn how to do these things for yourself, you'd better call **Tele-Close** at (617) 547-6372 to find out how we can help you!)

#R118

HOW TO QUALIFY YOUR NETWORK MARKETING LEADS, SO YOU'RE SPENDING YOUR TIME AND MONEY ONLY ON THE PEOPLE WHO JOIN YOUR ORGANIZATION. Every single day I hear from people who need this report desperately... people who are making cold calls, sending expensive mailing packages and otherwise shooting themselves in the foot. Here are the details you need on how to qualify your leads... so you're working only with people who are reasonable risks for what you're selling. Stop using cold calls! Stop sending expensive packages to people who will simply throw them away. This is the system I use... and it works. $7

#R121

IS YOUR MLM COMPANY INDEPENDENT DISTRIBUTOR FRIENDLY? GIVE IT THIS HANDY QUIZ AND FIND OUT FOR YOURSELF. *Before* you join any network marketing company, find out whether it makes sense. How? By giving your proposed company this quiz... and finding out whether it really makes sense to join them. $7

#R131

HOW I MAKE MORE MONEY EVERY MONTH WITH THE STAFF OF LIFE... WHAT YOU HAVE TO DO SO YOU WILL, TOO! Every single month, I make MORE MONEY from my involvement in The Staff of Life. Why? Because I follow an unrelenting *system* that ensures profit. Are you in network marketing now? Did you make substantially more money this month than last? If not, join me! Or, are you looking for a rock-solid *investment*, an opportunity which, if you work it properly, will pay off for you? If so, join me in The Staff of Life and follow these steps. $7

#R132

SHOULD YOU JOIN THE NEWEST 'HOT' NETWORK MARKETING PRO-GRAM? HERE ARE THE SENSIBLE GUIDELINES FOR YOU TO FOLLOW. If you sit in my office on any given day, you'll seek fax after fax come in, and offer after offer mailed in, of the new "hot" MLM opportunities. Come back in six months and most of them will be out of business, another expensive joke. I've become supremely cynical about these "opportunities" and disgusted by the way they seduce people into them. Should you get in? Follow my recommended scrutinizing devices and see for yourself. $7

#R133

Network marketer. If you're sitting on your backside complaining that your opportunity isn't working, it's time to join... **THE REVOLUTION OF PERSONAL RESPONSIBIL-ITY.** When I got into MLM, it never occurred to me that I wouldn't work hard, wouldn't develop a system, and wouldn't do everything necessary to ensure my success. I thought I'd find lots of people to share my old-fashioned beliefs about the necessity for hard work. But I was wrong! Too many parasites, too many pea-brained big talkers, too many liers and loafers. If you want to make money in MLM there are things you've got to do. Here they are. I suggest you make sure every member of your downline memorizes this report. Otherwise, chuck 'em. $7

#R134

HOW TO GET YOUR DOWNLINE TO PARTICIPATE IN YOUR ORGANIZA-TION AND BUY PRODUCT. It's utterly astonishing to me how many people are in MLM companies and don't feel compelled to buy the product. This is immoral. Here are the guidelines you need to make sure your people buy the product and fully participate in growing your organization. $7

#R135

ACTING LIKE THE NATIONAL SALES DIRECTOR OF YOUR NETWORK MAR-KETING ORGANIZATION! The "little guys" who like to think they're going to make their fortune in MLM make lots of mistakes. But one of the most stupid is failing to run even the tiniest organization like they were its national sales director. I run my group like the "Autocrat of the Breakfast Table" that I am. People have quotas, objectives, schedules, directions to follow. As a result, I get bigger checks monthly. Does it irk some people? Yes, the losers. But people who want to make money, understand that it takes a system to do so. Here's what you've got to do to achieve success. $7

#R136

HOW TO MAKE INCREASING MONTHLY INCOME FROM AMERICA'S EASI-EST NETWORK MARKETING OPPORTUNITY.... THE GOURMET COFFEE CLUB. I'm not like those witless boobs who tell you to only work one MLM program. No way. I sell health-minded people what *they* like and need (the 40+ products put out by The Staff of Life), recognizing that while everybody ought to be interested in improving their health, lots of people (as evidenced by the mess most people are in) don't care a fig about it. And I sell those interested in cashing in on the $11 billion coffee market what they want: 16 tasty gourmet flavors. Remember, over 100,000,000 Americans drink coffee every single day. You're never going to run out of prospects for this opportunity. It's the easiest I've ever promoted, and I'm personally signing up between 15-25 people every day, working just part time. $7

#R137

HOW YOUR NONPROFIT ORGANIZATION CAN PROFIT FROM THE GOURMET COFFEE CLUB: PRECISE STEPS YOU CAN TAKE RIGHT THIS MINUTE TO DERIVE INCREASING, UNRESTRICTED INCOME EVERY SINGLE MONTH! Nonprofit organizations have taken a beating in recent years. Lots of things have contributed to the fact that contributions are down for most of them. Traditional thinking and traditional means of fund raising are passé and are just not going to raise the amounts of money these organizations need. That's why nonprofits have got to tap into the massive economic power of this country, which means getting smart about getting a percentage of commodities sold. This includes coffee. I've developed an ingenious and simple system that virtually any nonprofit organization can use to raise unrestricted income. Here it is. $7

#R138

IF I HEAR "IT'S EASY FOR YOU, JEFFREY," ONE MORE TIME, I'LL SCREAM, OR THE REASON YOU'RE NOT SUCCESSFUL IN NETWORK MARKETING IS BECAUSE YOU'RE NOT PROGRAMMED FOR SUCCESS. I've been meaning to write this report for some time now. Why? Because every single day people use my success in network marketing as a means of excusing their own non-performance. "If I had your advantages, Jeffrey, I'd be as successful as you are." Well, here's my response. I've programmed myself for success and insist upon achieving it. If you absolutely insist upon becoming successful in MLM here's what you need to do so. And if you want to look for reasons why you can't succeed, get lost. $7

#R139

HOW I GET 10,000,000+ FREE POST CARDS EVERY YEAR TO BOOST MY MLM ORGANIZATIONS... HOW YOU CAN, TOO! One major reason why I'm so successful in business generally and in MLM in particular is because I use leverage — other people's money — to run millions of free post card yearly. My colleague and pal Robert Blackman and I are the most clever creators of advertising co-ops ever. We run a ton of them. Why? Because we generate tens of thousands of leads this way that help develop our organizations — and we don't pay a dime for the cards. Is this smart, or what? If you're anxious to achieve the really big success, you've got to become a co-op master. Here are the steps you need. $7

Note: want to participate in our Staff of Life, Gourmet Coffee Club and Ad-Net advertising co-ops for a reasonable price? Then call Robert directly at (405) 360-9487.

The Staff of Life

Independent Distributor Application

New Distributor	Enrolled By	Place Under (optional)
Name	Name **Lant/Blackman** **BETTER HEALTH TEAM**	Name
Address	Address **P.O. Box 38-2767**	Address
City, State, Zip	City, State, Zip **Cambridge, MA 02238**	City, State, Zip
Social Security Number	Distributor ID Number **18194**	Distributor ID Number
Phone	Phone **ph: (617) 547-6372**	Phone

Terms of This Agreement

1. I am of legal age in the state in which I enter this agreement.
2. As a Staff of Life Distributor, I acknowledge that I am an independent contractor and not an agent or employee of The Staff of Life.
3. I understand that no purchase other than a Distributor Manual is necessary to become a Staff of Life Distributor. I further understand that I am under no obligation to make any financial investment to become a Staff of Life Distributor.
4. I understand that in order to maintain a viable marketing system and to comply with the changes in applicable laws, The Staff of Life reserves the right to change prices, company policies and/or the marketing plan, without prior notice.
5. I agree to abide by the Company policies and procedures, as stated in this Agreement and in The Staff of Life Policies and Procedures Statement.

Applicant Signature	Date

☐ **Option 1 - Included with this application is $25 for my Complete Distributor Kit**
☐ **Option 2 - Included with this application is $5 for my Distributor Kit**

Payment by: ☐ Check ☐ Visa ☐ Mastercard ☐ Discover

Credit Card Number _____ Exp. Date _____

DISTRIBUTOR ORDER FORM

The Staff of Life

As a new Distributor you qualify immediately for these low prices!

Distributor I.D. # _____ Date _____

Name _____	Ship To (if different):	
Address _____	Name _____	
City, State, Zip _____	Address _____	
☐ Check ☐ Money Order ☐ Visa ☐ MasterCard ☐ Discover	City, State, Zip _____	Make all checks payable to: The Staff of Life
Credit Card Number _____ Exp. Date _____		

Quantity	Product	Size	Retail Price	Distributor Price	Total
*	L. Salivarius	30 capsules	$39.95	$24.00	
	L. Salivarius	90 capsules	$107.95	$65.00	
	L. Salivarius	180 capsules	$199.95	$125.00	
	L. Salivarius-Chewable	30 tablets	$39.95	$24.00	
	L. Salivarius-Chewable	90 tablets	$107.95	$65.00	
*	Multi Vitamin-Mineral Formula	90 capsules	$22.95	$14.00	
	Multi Vitamin-Mineral Formula	180 capsules	$44.95	$27.00	
	Multi Vitamin-Mineral Formula	360 capsules	$82.95	$50.00	
	Multi Vitamin-Mineral Formula	720 capsules	$157.95	$95.00	
*	Quadra-Zyme Plus	90 capsules	$24.95	$15.00	
	Quadra-Zyme Plus	180 capsules	$47.95	$29.00	
	Quadra-Zyme Plus	360 capsules	$92.95	$56.00	
	Quadra-Zyme Plus	720 capsules	$164.95	$100.00	
	Omni-Zyme	90 capsules	$17.95	$11.00	
	Omni-Zyme	180 capsules	$34.95	$21.00	
*	Bio-Synergy	10 ounces	$56.95	$34.00	
	Herbal Blend #1	1000 tablets	$141.95	$85.00	
	Gamma-Zyme	90 capsules	$17.95	$11.00	
	Gamma-Zyme	180 capsules	$34.95	$21.00	
	Amylase Formula	90 capsules	$17.95	$11.00	
	Amylase Formula	180 capsules	$34.95	$21.00	
	Lactose Formula	90 capsules	$24.95	$15.00	
	Lipase Formula	90 capsules	$17.95	$11.00	
	Lipase Formula	180 capsules	$34.95	$21.00	
	Protease Formula	90 capsules	$21.50	$13.00	
	Protease Formula	180 capsules	$41.50	$25.00	
	Milk Thistle Formula	90 capsules	$17.95	$11.00	
	Milk Thistle Formula	180 capsules	$34.95	$21.00	
	Anti-Oxidant Formula	90 capsules	$21.50	$13.00	
	Anti-Oxidant Formula	180 capsules	$41.50	$25.00	
	Pycnogenol Formula	90 capsules	$45.95	$28.00	
	Pycnogenol Formula	90 capsules	$89.95	$54.00	
*	Pycnogenol Prime 20 (20 mgs per tablet)	60 tablets	$24.95	$15.00	
	Pycnogenol Prime 20	180 tablets	$69.95	$42.00	
	Pycnogenol Prime 20	360 tablets	$130.00	$78.00	
	Silverfoid -- Colloidal Silver	4 ounces	$39.95	$24.00	
	Echinacea Formula	90 capsules	$21.50	$13.00	
	Ephedra Formula	90 capsules	$17.95	$11.00	
	Pau D'Arco Formula	90 capsules	$21.50	$13.00	
	Horsetail Formula	90 capsules	$21.50	$13.00	
	Bowel Toner NEW!	240 capsules	$44.95	$27.00	
*	Distributor Kit - Choose Kit Option 1 or 2			$25.00 or $5.00	

PRODUCT TOTAL	
Sales Tax (WA & CA)	
Handling	$4.00
Special Shipping	
Total Due:	

SPECIAL SHIPPING
Additional $3 for UPS Second Day Air
Additional $12 for UPS Next Day Air
Alaska & Hawaii $3 extra for Priority Mail, Canada $5 extra

ORDERING HOURS
7:30 a.m. till 5:00 p.m. Pacific Time, Monday thru Friday

SUBSCRIBER
APPLICATION / AGREEMENT

PLATINUM SUBSCRIBER (100 Leads per month plus FREE Voice Mail Service)

☐ Yes, I wish to become a Platinum Subscriber!

☐ Enclosed is $114 ($159 CD) for my first month's subscription including a $15 ($21 CD) one-time registration fee. I hereby authorize AD-NET to draft my $99 ($138 CD) subscription fee from my bank account each month, starting one month from the date my application is approved. I have enclosed a voided check which I understand is required to set up the draft program with my bank. If thereafter I become a Marketer, I authorize Ad-Net to deduct my $99 monthly subscription fee as a subscriber from my commission check at any month in which my monthly commission reaches $99.

☐ I do not wish to participate in the automatic draft program. I am enclosing $177 ($249 CD) for my first three month's subscription fees, plus my one-time registration fee of $15 ($21 CD). Total amount of $312 ($434 CD). If I should elect to discontinue my subscription before any pre-payment has expired, I understand that I will receive a refund of the unused portion of the pre-payment.

☐ I wish to become an AD-NET Marketer. I understand there is no fee or purchase required. Please RUSH my marketer application.

GOLD SUBSCRIBER (50 Leads per month)

☐ Yes, I wish to become a Gold Subscriber!

☐ Enclosed is $74 ($104 CD) for my first month's subscription including a $15 ($21 CD) one-time registration fee. I hereby authorize AD-NET to draft my $59 ($83 CD) subscription fee from my bank account each month, starting one month from the date my application is approved. I have enclosed a voided check which I understand is required to set up the draft program with my bank. If hereafter I become a Marketer, I authorize Ad-Net to deduct my $59 monthly subscription fee as a subscriber from my commission check at any month in which my monthly commission reaches $59.

☐ I do not wish to participate in the automatic draft program. I am enclosing $177 ($249 CD) for my first three month's subscription fees, plus my one-time registration fee of $15 ($21 CD). Total amount of $192 ($270 CD). If I should elect to discontinue my subscription before my pre-payment has expired, I understand that I will receive a refund of the unused portion of the pre-payment.

☐ I wish to become an AD-NET Marketer. I understand there is no fee or purchase required. Please RUSH my marketer application.

SILVER SUBSCRIBER (30 Leads per month)

☐ Yes, I wish to become a Silver Subscriber!

☐ Enclosed is $54 ($76CD) for my first month's subscription including a $15 ($21 CD) one-time registration fee. I hereby authorize AD-NET to draft my $39 ($55CD) subscription fee from my bank account each month, starting one month from the date my application is approved. I have enclosed a voided check which I understand is required to set up the draft program with my bank. If hereafter I become a Marketer, I authorize Ad-Net to deduct my $39 monthly subscription fee as a subscriber from my commission check at any month in which my commission reaches $39.

☐ I do not wish to participate in the automatic draft program. I am enclosing $117 ($165 CD) for my first three month's subscription fees, plus my one-time registration fee of $15 ($21 CD). Total amount of $132 ($186 CD). If I should elect to discontinue my subscription before my pre-payment has expired, I understand that I will receive a refund of the unused portion of the pre-payment.

☐ I wish to become an AD-NET Marketer. I understand there is no fee or purchase required. Please RUSH my marketer application.

You may cancel this agreement at any time regardless of reason.
Cancellation must be submitted in writing to AD-NET Inc. at its principal place of business.

Subscriber Information

Please Print or Type All Information Clearly and Accurately

Last Name _____ First _____ Middle Initial _____

Business Name _____

Address _____ OR Phone Number ( )_____

City _____ State _____ Zip Code _____

Social Security or Federal I.D. number _____

Legal Signature _____

Sponsor Information

Sponsor Information

Total Enclosed With This Application Payable to Ad-Net Inc.	$	Subscription effective upon receipt and acceptance at AD-NET's Headquarters	Lant	Dr. Jeffrey	4040
			Last Name	*First*	*ID Number*

Send Completed Application and Check(s) made payable to AD-NET INC. to:
Jim Wingo, President • Ad-Net, Inc. • 3227 Meade Ave. #3B • Las Vegas, NV 89102 • (702) 227-6655
Or Fax your application with a copy of a voided check to (702) 227-6383 Fax

---

AD-NET MARKETER COMPENSATION PLAN

Anyone may become an AD-NET marketer without cost or purchase. The primary responsibility of a marketer is to make personal subscription sales. A marketer's right to build and receive commissions from a downline organization of marketer's is conditioned upon the making of personal subscription sales. A marketer may earn commissions on his or her own subscription sales and on the subscription sales made by other marketers in his or her downline organization.

TRAINING SUBSIDY BONUS

The Training Subsidy Bonus (TSB) will allow a new marketer to earn a total monthly commission of $39 by enrolling only 2 subscribers. This bonus is designed to equal the monthly AD-NET subscription fee. If the marketer is also a Silver subscriber, his/her subscription fee is covered after 2 subscriptions have been sold.

FOR EXAMPLE: If the marketer has personally enrolled 2 subscribers, he or she would receive a monthly commission of $4 for each and a TSB of $34 for a total commission of $42 minus a $3 processing fee, or a total net commission of $39. If the marketer has personally enrolled 2 subscribers and has a total of 5 subscribers in his/her downline, he/she would receive a monthly commission of $20 and a TSB of $22 (total net commission of $39). Another way of looking at this is that once you have personally enrolled 2 new subscribers, AD-NET will actually pay you in advance for your 3rd, 4th, 5th, 6th, 7th, 8th, 9th, and 10th subscribers. The TSB is in effect for a period of 6 months from the marketers entry date.

SPECIAL PLATINUM BONUS

Downline commissions on our $99 subscription will be the same as our $59 plan. HOWEVER, EACH PERSONALLY ENROLLED $99 SUBSCRIBER WILL EARN THE ENROLLER A MONTHLY BONUS COMMISION OF $31 PLUS REGULAR DOWNLINE COMMISSION OF EITHER $4 OR $8.

The $99 plan will also pay a $70 fast start commission on all new $99 subscribers and on $39 and $59 subscribers who upgrade to the $99 plan.

Level	Potential Subscribers	Monthly Payout Gold	Silver	Requirements
1	3	$4.00 /	$4.00	$39 Personal Volume (PV)
2	9	$4.00 /	$4.00	$39 PV
3	27	$4.00 /	$4.00	$39 PV
4	81	$4.00 /	$4.00	Maintain or upgrade to $59 PV
5	243	$4.00 /	$4.00	$59 PV & Maintain 3 Active PES†
6	729	$8.00 /	$4.00	$59 PV & Maintain 5 Active PES†
7	2187	$8.00 /	n/a	*Executive Director
8	6561	$8.00 /	n/a	**Senior Executive Director

*Executive Director Qualifications: Maintain a monthly PV of $99 and a total of 100 active subscribers on levels 1 through 6

**Senior Executive Director Qualifications: Maintain a monthly PV of $99 and a total 7 level Group Volume (GV) of $20,000

THE PLATINUM SUBSCRIBER

As a Platinum Subscriber you will receive 100 leads each month, 3 FREE ad certificates (value up to $35) & Voice Mail Service in exchange for a monthly subscription fee of $99 ($138 CD).

THE GOLD SUBSCRIBER

As a Gold Subscriber you will receive 50 leads each month and 2 FREE ad certificates (value up to $25) in exchange for a monthly subscription fee of $59 ($83 CD).

THE SILVER SUBSCRIBER

As a Silver Subscriber you will receive 30 leads each month and 1 FREE ad certificate (value up to $15) in exchange for a monthly subscription fee of $39 ($55 CD).

FAST-START COMMISSIONS

A marketer will receive a $21 Fast Start Commission for each Silver Subscription sold, a $40 Fast Start Commission for each Gold Subscription sold and a $70 Fast Start Commission for each Platinum Subscription sold. Fast Start commissions represent the entire first month's commissions paid on a new subscription. Regular upline commissions are earned starting with the second subscription month.

Fast Start commissions are paid on the 1st and 16th of each month and begin with the 3rd Silver or Gold subscription sold or with the 1st Platinum subscription sold.

If a marketer is not a subscriber he/she must enroll at least one new marketer each month in order to qualify for commissions.

PES = Personally Enrolled Subscribers

Tele-Close

Want help calling your network marketing (MLM) prospects?

No time? Hate the phone?
NO PROBLEM!!!

Now Let Dr. Jeffrey Lant's Tele-Close Lead-Calling Service Help You Build Your Profitable MLM Organization!!!

At Tele-Close . . .

. . .we know how you may either hate calling or simply don't have the time after a hard day's work. No problem! Our job at Tele-Close is to help you sort through your leads and find those people who are really interested in joining your program!

We do not claim to build your downline for you. And we cannot promise to close every prospect you send us. What we do promise is to call each of your prospects up to 3 times and to try to eliminate all procrastinators, time wasters and tire kickers, etc.

When we do find a prospect who is interested, we either mail you a report or call/fax you immediately for a hot lead. And if you are an Ad-Net member we will talk to them about joining both your program AND Ad-Net at NO EXTRA CHARGE!!! Get the benefit of two calls for the price of only one!

- Interested in Card-Decks or
- Lead-Generator Programs?
- Call Jeffrey At (617) 547-6372

Join Ad-Net for at least 30 prospect leads monthly.

In Dr. Lant's Ad-Net organization already? Participate in our Ad-Net card-deck co-op programs! Call Robert Blackman at (405) 360-9487.

Here's how you can benefit from Tele-Close

1. Gather your prospect leads any way you want. (Remember, we can help you through our card-deck; Nationwide Lead-Generator Program.)

2. Once you've got your leads, determine how many of them you want Tele-Close to call for you. Send us a complete list of prospects with name, address & phone #, writing carefully or (preferable) typing all necessary information.

3. Add a one-time only fee of $35 to activate your relationship with Tele-Close.

4. Send in the completed form with applicable payment (see right) to:
Robert Blackman
ATTN: Tele-Close
P.O. Box 1390,
Norman, OK 73070

5. Once Tele-Close has received your leads, you will be contacted as soon as we find you a hot prospect! Then you can either call or mail them your program's marketing material.

> Do not send any information to any prospects before sending us your leads!!! Remember, our objective is to have you call or mail only those prospects who have told us they are interested in your program or Ad-Net. Let us do the sorting & sifting -- you concentrate on closing them into your organization!!

6. You will receive a detailed report on all calls made on your behalf by Tele-Close, contacts made, and future action indicated.

☎ ☎ ORDER DETAILS ☎ ☎

SEND IN
1) this form with $35 activation fee if applicable
2) payment for leads
3) list of prospects with all available lead information including name, complete address and phone numbers
AND 4) a self-addressed stamped envelope for our report.

☐ **OPTION 1** – I have enclosed $ _____ to call _____ # of leads @ $3 per lead. I am a member of _____ AND Dr. Jeffrey Lant's Ad-Net organization and I want Tele-Close to call prospects about BOTH programs.

☐ **OPTION 2** – I have enclosed $ _____ to call _____ # of leads @ $4 per lead. I am a member of _____ but NOT the Dr. Jeffrey Lant Ad-Net team, so I only want Tele-Close to call these leads about my program.

☐ Check   ☐ MC   ☐ Visa   ☐ Amex   ☐ Discover

Card # _____ Exp. _____

Signature _____

Name _____

Address _____

City, _____ St _____ Zip _____

Day Phone _____

Eve. Phone _____

☎ ☎ ☎ ☎ ☎ ☎ ☎ ☎ ☎ ☎

Questions? Call Robert Blackman
(405) 360-9487 10-6 CST

Send Order To: Robert Blackman • P.O. Box 1390 • Norman, OK 73070

Dr. Jeffrey Lant's Money Mall

Would You Pay Pennies A Day To Make Your Full Page Ad Available To Over 30 Million People?

It doesn't matter if you own a home based business or are a corporate CEO —you will make money by having your own Home Page in our Money Mall.

Of course you would! Let us design a Home Page for *your* company and market it on the World Wide Web—and you can start making money by being a part of Dr. Jeffrey Lant's Money Mall. The future of marketing is in on-line marketing. Over 30 million people are already logged onto the Internet, with over 1 million more joining per month. The World Wide Web is the fastest growing media forum in the *world*. If you aren't already on the Internet, you can be sure your competitors are! Now is the time to start building your profits through this global medium. At Jeffrey Lant's Money Mall, we help you turn the Internet into an unrelenting marketing tool. Reach consumers around the world for literally pennies a day!! All day... every day! Yes, you can make money while you're sleeping!

Let Us Put You On The World Wide Web!

♦Users of the Internet are an upscale consumer base of over 30 million people around the globe—a rapidly growing group of consumers who are educated, computer literate, affluent and motivated!

♦The Home Pages we create are unique, exciting, interactive and profitable! Customers who visit your Home Page can choose what information they would like to see and tour your business, including company and product information, price lists, order forms, specials, bonuses—things that will entice the customer to *buy*. And—we can even make it possible for customers to order *instantly* when they come to your Home Page!

♦Our Fax on Demand service can't be beat. Information such as product order forms and sign-up information can be made available to people who visit your Home Page. This timely delivery of information will provide your customers with immediate access to you 24 hours a day, 7 days a week!

♦Compare our **low cost** for a Home Page to other more expensive media forms with a fraction of the exposure. Some companies selling Home Pages charge as much as $750 per month and $1.50 per lead extra! *Our prices are unbelievably low by comparison* — the lowest in the industry!!!

♦We save you time, money and frustration by eliminating the hassle of learning how to do it yourself. We do the all the work. You can just sit back and wait for your **'Profit Page'** to make money for you!

♦In MLM? You'll be the *only* one who can use your opportunity's name!

♦We aggressively promote the Money Mall to millions worldwide. There's no point in being part of any Mall or Home Page that isn't *aggressively promoted like*

You Get These Great Benefits!

- We will set up your Home Page, usually within 24 hours.
- An opportunity to make available your company's message to millions of people every single day.
- International exposure without the enormous cost associated with traditional expensive forms of advertising.
- Special Fax on Demand service for Mall participants!!

Our low introductory prices WILL go up SO ACT NOW!!

If you're on the Internet then e-mail: incor@supernet.ab.ca, or check out the Money Mall at: http://www.supernet.ab.ca/Mall/Business/incor/lantmall.htm

Choose **One** Of These Methods To Get Us The Materials We Need To Get You Started!

- Fax your typed information to us at (403) 479-6988. Your Home Page can be up in 24 hours, in most cases!
- E-mail the text you want included in your Home Page to: incor@supernet.ab.ca. We will convert your message to HTML and create your Home Page! (IBM files only)
- Mail an IBM disk or typed page to WorldProfit, Suite 304, 11807-101 Street, Edmonton, Alberta, Canada T5G 2B6
- If selecting Option 2 or the Deluxe Option with Fax on Demand service, mail your documents (maximum of 3) to WorldProfit at the above address.

Choose one of the payment options below to enclose with your information. When your material is received, we will contact you about the details of your Home Page and/or the Fax on Demand service.

Your Basic Home Page Includes:

1. Professional consultation from experienced computer programmers.
2. 125 lines of text.
3. Your own unique World Wide Web address.
4. FREE e-mail link to your Home Page.
5. Registration with over 12 search computers.
6. FREE 10 page report on making Internet $.
7. FREE 60-character ad promoting your Home Page (100,000 circ) — if you take one-year contract!

Our Fax on Demand Service

Allows you to provide up to 3 pages of information 24 hours a day, seven days a week. This low cost service is available *only* to participants in the Money Mall!

There is a one-time set-up fee for the following **optional** Home Page customization features

- Additional Pages –$15 per page
- Button Graphics –$5 each
- Graphical Dividers –$5 each
- Hyperlinks to Other Sites –$2 each
- Scanned logo or graphic –$65

For More Information About Reserving Your Exclusive Space
Call Jeffrey's Personal Representative George Kosch at: (403) 471-6308

PAYMENT OPTIONS
(Please Note: All Prices in US Dollars)

❑ OPTION 1 – I want my Home Page to run for six months. Enclosed is $99.95.

❑ OPTION 2 – I want my Home Page to run for six months and profit from the Fax on Demand service. $169.95.

❑ OPTION 3 – I want my Home Page to run for twelve months and receive a FREE 60 character line on the "InternetConnect Card" (circulation 100,000). $179.95.

❑ DELUXE OPTION – I want my Home Page to run for twelve months and profit from the Fax on Demand service. $279.95. YOU SAVE $149.88!

Please send your check or money order to: (make payable to WorldProfit)

WorldProfit, Inc.
Suite 304, 11807-101 St.
Edmonton, Alberta T5G 2B6, Canada
Ph: (403) 471-6308 or Fax: (403) 479-6988

❑ Check ❑ Money Order ❑ MC/Visa

Card # _____ Exp:_____

Signature_____

Name_____

Address_____

City_____

Prov/State_____PC/Zip_____

Phone ( )_____

Fax ( )_____

Name of Company Reservation (first come basis)

_____

Jeffrey Lant Associates, Inc.

50 Follen Street, Suite 507
Cambridge, MA 02138

Phone: (617) 547-6372 • Fax: (617) 547-0061

ADVERTISER:

Name_____

Title_____

Company_____

Address_____

City_____

State _____ Zip_____

Phone ( )_____

Fax ( )_____

Signature _____

Please Reserve_____card(s) at $_____
in the_____issue of the
JLA Sales & Marketing SuccessDek.
❐ Payment enclosed ❐ Payment will be sent on _____

CARD SPECIFICATIONS:

This Card is: (check only one)

❐ Blue   ❐ Green   ❐ Purple   ❐ Red

❐ 4-Color   ❐ Black & White   ❐ Other_____

The publisher will try to accommodate your color request but in the event that space is not available for the color you selected reserves the right to change the color.

CAMERA-READY ART:

❐ is enclosed as:

   ❐ Film   ❐ Laser Copy   ❐ Mechanical

   ❐ Photo/Art: __Bl.&Wh. __4-Color __Other

❐ is on file with Jeffrey Lant Associates
      Deck Issue/Code#_____

❐ must be picked up from another printer:

Important: If artwork is to be picked up from another source you must specify below the name of the publisher, name of the deck, key code on the card, printer if known, and fax a copy of both sides of the card to be inserted to (617) 547-0061.

Publisher:_____
Name of Deck:_____
Key Code: _____
Printer:_____

CORRECTIONS/ADDITIONS:

Please indicate clearly any changes or revisions required to update your current artwork or film (these changes will be billed accordingly):_____

_____

_____

_____

_____

Jeffrey Lant Associates, Inc.

50 Follen Street, Suite 507
Cambridge, MA 02138

Phone: (617) 547-6372 • Fax: (617) 547-0061

JLA Lead-Generator Program runs a card in the Jeffrey Lant Sales & Marketing SuccessDek. This deck reaches 100,000 people nationwide every 90 days.

JLA will prepare the card, print, publish and distribute 100,000 cards, collect prospect information, and disseminate all prospect information acquired to advertiser at regular intervals.

JLA will print all leads on laser sheets with name, address, city, state, zip and phone number (if given). Leads will be mailed twice monthly until the next card deck mails.

Advertiser may run more than one listing at a time. Simply photocopy this form and send 60 characters and $90 for each listing advertiser wants listed.

Advertiser will submit copy of not more than 60 characters and $90 as full payment for each listing.

INSERTION ORDER

JLA Lead-Generator Program

ADVERTISER:

Name _____

Title _____

Company _____

Street Address _____

City _____

State _____ Zip _____

Business Phone ( ) _____

Fax ( ) _____

Authorized Signature _____

(Insert ad copy above. 60 character maximum including spaces & punctuation)
Please type, print, or include separate sheet.

I want to run _____ listing(s). Total payment of $_____ ($90 x # of listings) is included.
Card Deck to run in: ❏ Jan. ❏ April ❏ July ❏ Oct.
❏ **Save $40!** Buy 4 issues or 1 Year (400,000 circulation) for only $320!

Advertiser Payment Options

I prefer to pay the one-time only insertion charge of $90 for each listing in the following way:

❏ Check (payable to Jeffrey Lant Associates, Inc.)

❏ Money Order

❏ Credit Card

    ❏ Visa ❏ MasterCard ❏ AMEX

Name on Card _____

Card Number _____

Expiration Date _____

Signature _____

This insertion order is a legally binding contract between the advertiser and publisher. Any changes made to this agreement are not valid unless agreed to in writing by Jeffrey Lant Associates Inc. (JLA Inc.) and the advertiser. This agreement supersedes and takes precedence to all other orders submitted for this account. Jeffrey Lant Associates, Inc. does not recognize agency discounts. All agency commissions must be paid by the advertiser and shall alter in no way the insertion price agreed to by this order. Once the insertion order is signed by the advertiser, no cancellations will be accepted without the explicit agreement of JLA Inc. JLA Inc. reserves the right to substitute another advertiser's advertisement if the essential materials are not received by the closing date, or re-run a previous advertisement. All advertising is subject to publisher's approval. Advertisers purchasing advertising in any JLA Inc. publication agree to protect and indemnify the publisher from any claims for libel, copyright violation, plagiarism, or privacy and other suits or claims based on the content or subject matter of such publication. Advertiser agrees to reimburse publisher for any legal fees under this agreement. Advertiser agrees to send payment with advertisement.